NEVER GIVE UP HOPE

WAGING WAR WITH CANCER

By Craig Davis

Called Writers Christian Publishing

Never Give Up Hope: Waging War With Cancer

Written by Craig Davis

Edited by Chris McKinney

Designed by Chris McKinney

Published by Called Writers Christian Publishing, LLC

ISBN 978-0-578-45599-0

First, this book is dedicated to God, the Lord Jesus, and the Holy Spirit. Without God, none of the things I've written about in this book would have been possible. Jesus made a way for me to receive supernatural healing. Without His love and compassion displayed on the cross, I would not be here. The Holy Spirit comforted me and helped me write down this story. I pray His presence is felt throughout the reading of this book.

To my wife, Casey: You are my inspiration. Your unfailing love and care for me throughout this journey have been immeasurable. You are the perfect example of a godly wife.

To my children, Alyssa, Tristen, Juliana, Gabby, Jaxson, and Owen: One day I hope you read this and understand the sacrifices you all have made.

To my friends and family: Your prayers and support have gotten us through this trial. I pray you know the impact you have made for the Kingdom of God.

Foreword

"Give thanks to the Lord and proclaim his greatness. Let the whole world know what he has done." – Psalm 105:1 (NLT)

When God does something great for us, He wants us to talk about it. He wants us to tell someone. That's the reason for this book. This is a story about faithfulness and courage—the faithfulness of a great God, and the courage of a young family to keep trusting Him no matter the circumstances.

We have had the privilege of walking part of this journey with Craig and his family, and of seeing them continue to stand in hope and faith. They have inspired our church family with their determination to trust God in the most challenging of circumstances.

It has also been wonderful to see how God has come through for them in their darkest moments. God is faithful, and He has proven that to Craig and his family again and again during their difficult journey.

I believe that Craig's story will inspire you as much as it has us—inspire you to never give up no matter what you face and inspire you to find new strength from God during your times of trial and challenge.

I pray that you will find in this story a new hope you didn't think possible.

Pastor Rick Hufton
Faith Family Church
Shiloh, Illinois

Preface

I pray that my story finds its way into the hands of everyone out there who is looking for hope. Maybe you just received bad news from the doctor, and you're googling "miracle healing from cancer." Maybe you're researching whether it's possible to have children after cancer treatment. Inside you are probably reeling and hurting. You may feel alone. You may even feel like God has abandoned you.

I am believing that the Holy Spirit reveals to you that God is a faithful, trustworthy Father. The Bible says: *"For you did not receive the spirit of bondage again to fear, but you received the Spirit of adoption, by whom we cry out 'Abba, Father.'"* – Romans 8:15 (NKJV)

You have a good, good Father in Heaven. I believe we live in a fallen world and that our enemy, Satan, uses disease, disasters, and tragedies to put doubt between you and a Father that loves you. As you read my testimony, please keep this in mind: If He did it before, He can do it again.

I am going to tell the story with my life as the backdrop. Though, the reality is this is a story about the goodness and faithfulness of God displayed throughout my simple, humble existence. There have been medical miracles which left my cancer doctors speechless and shaking their heads. However, the real story is a faith journey filled with peaks and valleys. The valleys tested my faith and ultimately led to a deep, intimate relationship with Jesus. The newfound intimacy I have with Him makes the entire journey well worth it. Throughout my journey I can look back at the milestones in my life and see God's hand molding me and shaping me into the man He desires for me to be. He is the potter, and I am the clay.

Acknowledgments

Special thanks to Chris McKinney for his phenomenal editing and advice throughout this process. It has been invaluable, and this testimony would not be documented without his help in putting this all together.

Also, we are very grateful to Dyane Forde for lending us her writing and editing talents on the Introduction. You are an amazing writer and person who deserves every good thing God is sending your way.

We deeply appreciate the prayer team: Shari, Janis, Ranae, Niki, Emmanuel, and others who covered this effort with prayer for many weeks. Your reward is eternal.

Last but not least, thank you to all the readers out there, especially the advance readers who offered feedback, insight, encouragement, and support to make this effort the best it could possibly be. You are greatly appreciated!

An Important Notice From the Publisher

Craig's book contains screenshots and URLs of Facebook posts that he and his family made while walking through the story you are about to read. The posts are generally very readable and easy to understand. Out of consideration for the reader, a few glaring typos in the original posts have been corrected.

However, beyond those few typos, the posts are completely unedited. They have not been edited for grammar, punctuation, capitalization, content, writing style, etc. The posts were written by people who were often sleep deprived, in pain, and living out of hospitals or other medical facilities. The unedited posts provide complete transparency to the reader.

There is something to be said for the value of carefully edited writing. In general, it can increase clarity and lead to fewer distractions for the reader. However, when everything was considered, it was determined that the Facebook posts should be left intact as they were originally written and posted.

Thank you for your understanding.

Table of Contents

Introduction:
"Something's Wrong"

Maxwell Air Force Base
Montgomery, Alabama

It's late 2009, and a young, hopeful Airman is realizing his dream of becoming an officer in the United States Air Force. The training is grueling, but he sticks with it, pushing himself to the limit. One day, at Officer Training School, he notices that his right thumb trembles when he salutes. That's odd, but he's twenty-nine years old and in peak physical condition. He shakes it off.

Time passes, and he begins to struggle with uncharacteristic fatigue. He also feels slightly dizzy when popping up from a round of push-ups. He assumes it must be the physical demands, stress, and irregular schedule that accompanies a military training environment. After all, the program is designed to challenge candidates mentally and physically.

The young man decides to push through.

Warner Robins, Georgia
Saturday, January 9th, 2010

Having recently completed Officer Training School, the newly commissioned Air Force Officer is a Second Lieutenant in the 52ⁿᵈ Combat Comm Squadron. While enjoying the weekend, he decides to put in a good workout with his wife at the local gym. Afterward, they head home to put their one-year-old daughter down for a nap.

Since the workout, the young officer has been feeling dizzy and decides he's not up for much else besides watching a movie. When he stands to put in the DVD, he suddenly falls to the floor. He's feeling extremely nauseous and has no idea why. He begins to vomit repeatedly. Frightened, his wife runs into the living room and helps him to bed.

The young officer vomits every time he moves. The dizziness is overwhelming; he can't make even the slightest movement without throwing up. So, he tries to lie still and focus his attention on the Alabama-LSU basketball game as a way to cope. But the back and forth of the game only makes him feel worse. Eventually, he decides he must have a terrible stomach virus—something foreign and exotic, the kind you normally only hear about on the news—and resolves to tough it out. But his wife is worried, and she calls for an ambulance instead.

The paramedics recommend that she take him to the hospital. There isn't much they can do for him anyway and, this way, she'd save some money. So, she loads the young officer into their Ford Bronco, and they head to the hospital located a few miles away.

The young officer arrives at the ER. He tells the doctor he thinks he has a stomach virus, but he can see from the doctor's eyes that he has a different hypothesis.

The doctor orders a CAT scan.

The young officer and his wife wait for the results...

CHAPTER ONE: Early Life

Hello, friend. I'm Craig, the young officer you just read about. My story actually begins much earlier in Northport, Alabama. Our family—which consisted of my parents, my younger brother, and me—moved there when I was five years old.

It was 1986. Halley's Comet was passing over the earth and Johnny Depp was passing up the role of Ferris Bueller. *Top Gun*, *Stand by Me*, and *Howard the Duck* were all big hits at the box-office. Most of us probably weren't aware of it at the time, but the Human Genome Project was being created and my dad, Rick Davis, had just graduated from the New Orleans Baptist Seminary.

I had a wonderful childhood growing up as a pastor's son in a small community just outside of Tuscaloosa—home of the Crimson Tide. I had plenty of friends in my neighborhood, and I took advantage of it. We played after school from the time we got home until dark. The most significant event of my childhood was my parents divorcing when I was in the 3rd grade. The divorce was painful for my parents and me. I ended up living with my dad and spending weekends and summers with my mom.

She eventually moved back to her hometown, a small town outside of Montgomery, where she remarried. I spent portions of my summers and every other holiday there with her. Most of her family lived within a few miles of each other, and I got to experience life on a farm in a rural community.

My granddad was a farmer and a cotton man. He showed me what hard work looks like. I spent long days with him battling the summer heat out in pea patches and corn fields. Life there was slower, and some days you just had to invent things to do. I have serious doubts as to whether my kids would have made it through those long summer days. But I suppose we all learn to rise to whatever situation life throws at us.

Eventually, my dad met someone too. A lady moved in next door and they began to date. I wasn't very happy about it at the time. I was selfish and didn't want anyone else taking away my dad's time and attention. They got married when I was in the 6th grade. It was a package deal, coming complete with a new brother and sister. I was now the oldest of four kids. Of course, life in a blended family presented its fair share of challenges. But now I look back, and I'm grateful for our expanded family and proud of the growth that has taken place.

I was a sports fanatic and still am today. Growing up, I played baseball and basketball year-round from little league through high school and anytime I could grab a pick-up game with friends. This was when I developed a deep love and passion for the Alabama Crimson Tide in all sports—but especially football. It's like love for Bama is baked into our food in Tuscaloosa. It somehow gets into our DNA and becomes part of us. Bama won the 1992 national championship against the Miami Hurricanes when I was 12 years old, and my devotion to the team was set in stone. All in all, I would say I had a relatively healthy and normal childhood, especially by today's standards.

My rebellious period somehow coincided with getting my own car at the age of 15. It was a blue, straight-shift, 1995 Ford Probe. They were sporty little cars, and mine even had a spoiler on the back. I was ready to do life my own way and have some fun. I no longer wanted to be the good preacher's kid. Instead, I idolized other kids that smoked cigarettes, cussed, and had a bad guy image.

My CD case was full of Nirvana, Pearl Jam, and Metallica, and I did my best to live out the rebellious attitude those guys displayed in their music. I was open to trying just about anything at any time. I still managed to get decent grades, but I just wanted to fit in with the people I thought were the cool crowd. I smoked cigarettes, weed, and tried sneaking out to go to parties. Basically, I was keen to pursue all attitudes, actions, and behaviors that clearly violated the rules of our home.

The Bible teaches that God works all things together for the good of those that love Him and are called according to His purpose. I can't say I loved God yet, but He was already working for my good. Ironically, it was my rule-breaking habits that God used to bring the first major change into my life. I had a terrible habit of keeping movies way past their due date. In the summer before my senior year, I rented a VHS from the local gas station. As usual the movie was way past due.

Around that time, I was hanging out at a friend's house one day in my neighborhood. He mentioned that a female friend was going to drop by and that she had a friend with her. The friend happened to work at the gas station where I had rented the movie. When they got there, I was instantly attracted to this girl, even though I had never met her before. She told me she could take the movie back for me and I wouldn't have to pay the late fees.

I was normally shy when it came to girls, but as soon as they left I was trying to track down her phone number. I wanted to call her right then and ask her out on a date. I didn't know it at the time, but she was doing the same thing—even going through the old White Pages phone book looking for my number. I tracked down her number and called, asking if she wanted to go swimming with me.

We lived near a lake, so my request wasn't anything out of the ordinary. But I confess that my primary motivation was to see her in a swimsuit because I thought she was smoking hot. Little did I know that this meeting would change the course of my life. God was at work, and we did not even recognize it.

From the time of our first date, Casey and I were inseparable. Interestingly enough, we were in church most every Sunday despite our lifestyle. I grew up in a home where you were at church on Sundays unless you were actively bleeding. On Sunday, November 16th 1997, our lives were changed eternally. The Holy Spirit weighed heavy on us, and we were convicted of our sin. We asked Jesus for forgiveness and gave our lives to Him.

The same day, we were both baptized new creations in Jesus. The Holy Spirit came to live inside of us, guaranteeing our salvation. Looking back, it feels like unseen forces determined at that point to get us to mess our lives up. There were strong temptations to continue sinning and making mistakes. We went through a few years of struggle as we ran from the life God was calling us to live.

CHAPTER TWO:
Getting Married and Enlisting

In January of 1998, we found out that we were going to be parents. We were very young, but we knew that we truly loved each other, so we decided to get married before the baby was born. We thought Valentine's Day would be perfect. We had no idea what we were getting into, and of course, everyone doubted whether things would work out in the long run. After all, we were both seventeen years old at the time and still in high school.

I graduated high school that May and provided for our young family by waiting tables and driving vending machine routes and delivery routes for Frito Lay. We had Alyssa in October of that year and added a son, Tristen, in August of 2000. Our lives were still a mess. Drinking and drug use caused us to have no sense of direction for our lives and led to marital strife. I was jealous of the people I was hanging out with because I felt like they had total freedom to do whatever they wanted. At that time, I did not yet understand true freedom.

In February of 2003, Casey and I separated. I felt completely lost spiritually and emotionally. I ended up in Hattiesburg, MS, working midnight shifts at a gas station just off the interstate. I was living with my mom, who was going through similar issues in her life after her husband had tragically passed away. I was 22 years old, running from my responsibilities as a husband and father. Most of all, I was running from the life Jesus wanted me to live. But God kept after me.

Late one night, my dad's friend showed up at the gas station where I was working. He came into the store acting drunk, and I knew he didn't even drink, so I thought the situation was odd. I called my dad to tell him what was going on and while we were on the phone, he came into the store laughing. They had driven over three hours to see me and tell me that God had not given up on me. They wanted me to know there was still hope to get my life back on track. After thinking about the situation I had put myself in, I came home a few days later with a renewed sense of purpose. I was ready to make something of my life.

My younger brother, Brad, had just graduated from Air Force boot camp and was home for his visit before going to tech school. We went camping and talked about the benefits of service and what basic training was like. It sounded doable to me. I figured if my younger brother could do it, then so could I.

I visited a recruiter and got a waiver for having two children. After taking the ASVAB, I qualified for a job as a computer programmer and got a date to leave for basic training in July of 2003. God had brought about another major change in my life by getting me into the Air Force. I was going to have a great job, and my hope in the future was restored. Next, God was going to work on my marriage and family.

While I was in tech school at Keesler Air Force Base, Casey and I reconnected over the phone, then eventually with in-person visits. The base was only about a 5-hour drive from her. I spent Christmas break with her and the kids. During the 6 months prior to us reconnecting, I had been trying to sabotage our marriage. But thank God, she eventually forgave me for all the terrible things I had done.

On New Year's Eve of 2003, we had a service to renew our vows at my dad's church. We call it our second anniversary. After that, we set off for Scott Air Force Base, which is right outside of St. Louis, but actually located in St. Clair County, Illinois. We went there for my first duty station and a restart on life.

CHAPTER THREE: Air Force Life and My Dreams

Unfortunately, not much changed as far as our habits during the first few years at Scott. We were still drinking and partying, but gradually things began to change. We were now living away from old stomping grounds and bad habits we had developed back in Tuscaloosa. Those habits had not been satisfying and were only causing us strife. They certainly weren't fun anymore. It was like the Holy Spirit said, "Enough."

The change in our environment was beneficial for us. I was in a good unit, and we had awesome neighbors. Our daughter, Alyssa, even attended church with them occasionally, and they were inviting us to go. Alyssa also kept asking us to go. The church was Faith Family Church in Shiloh, Illinois.

They had just built a new facility. It was big compared to what I was used to back home, so I thought it would be much easier to blend in. I wouldn't feel like every eye was on me the way I did at my dad's church. It turns out that I had many misconceptions about what it was like to live a Christian life. The Holy Spirit did not let me blend in or hide in the back row for very long.

All of a sudden, our lives became very busy. Our family was growing. We had another baby in February of 2006, a little girl we named Juliana. I was taking as many evening classes as I could at the local community college. Work was going great, and we had become active in the church. Once that happened, we were able to leave old habits behind for good.

The church was non-denominational and the pastors, Rick and Marjie Hufton, are great teachers of the Scripture. I was volunteering in the nursery, in the 1st through 3rd-grade class, and with some inner-city missions. Jesus became the center of our lives and our marriage. Casey and I were introduced to the baptism of the Holy Spirit and received our prayer language. I was actively seeking God's will for my life, and everything was heading in the right direction. I thought we were doing all we could for Jesus, but we were just scratching the surface.

There were a couple of events which did not seem as significant then as they do now. In the summer of 2005, while at a women's retreat, Casey had a vision of me in a hospital bed being wheeled away to surgery. In 2008, I had an extremely vivid dream. In my dream, I saw a person I believed to be Jesus. He approached me and told me I had a tumor and that it had to be removed. The dream really messed with me since up to that point in time, I had not had any prophetic dreams or visions.

I emailed my dad about the dream and asked if he could share it with a lady in his church who might be able to interpret it for me. After some back and forth, we decided that the dream just meant that there was something in my life that needed to be changed. I wrote the "tumor" off as possibly being symbolic of a hidden sin because I was dealing with issues around pornography. There were other possible explanations we considered at the time, but later events would reveal how the Holy Spirit was actually preparing us for what was to come.

Maybe there is also a lesson about struggles with willful sin. It can sometimes cloud our judgment and may affect our ability to hear and understand what the Lord is saying. Either way, I would definitely recommend that if God gives anyone a message, always fully consider the literal interpretation first. If the literal meaning is ruled out, then consider symbolic interpretations.

Late in 2008, we welcomed another child into the world. This time, we had a little red-headed girl and named her Gabriella, or Gabby for short. Now we were a family of six, with three daughters and one son. I was still active duty Air Force, and I was now going to school at Saint Louis University as much as I could. We also continued to stay active at church. I loved my life in the Air Force and developed a strong desire to become an officer and make it my career. After graduating with my Bachelor of Science degree in 2009, I applied for Officer Training School.

I had developed many friendships at church, at work, and in the community. Our lives were going extremely well. Our family was growing. I had graduated college and achieved a dream that I wouldn't have previously thought possible: I was selected to become an officer in our country's great Air Force.

It took a lot of hard work on my part as well as my family sacrificing a lot of time with their husband and daddy. I had a few contractors trying to recruit me, and I saw how much money my friends who had separated from service were making. As much as I wanted to be an officer, the possibility of more money for less demanding work was enticing. So, I decided I needed to take time alone to pray about the decision and seek the Holy Spirit's direction.

There is a place in central Missouri called Line Camp Cabin. I found it online, and it was exactly what I was looking for. The one-room cabin had no electricity and was in the middle of nowhere, deep in the Ozark hills. I spent two nights there praying, walking the hills, and going out on the small river in a canoe, all the while contemplating this momentous decision in our lives.

If I forged ahead with Officer Training School, I would be committing my family to a life of frequent moving, deployments, and living a military lifestyle. On the flip side, we could stay in a place we had grown to love. We'd be there with our friends and our church home. And I would have a great job, making more money than I could have imagined while driving that Frito Lay truck years ago. While it went against our natural desires to some degree, I felt like God was clearly telling me to accept the appointment to OTS.

Officer Training School was a 17-week course at Maxwell Air Force Base in Montgomery, Alabama. Soon after accepting the appointment to OTS, we found out that my next duty assignment would be at Robins Air Force Base. Since my new permanent base was only three hours from where I would be training, we went ahead and bought our first home and moved down to Warner Robins, Georgia. Leaving the lives we had built in Saint Louis was tough. We had made great friends, and we loved the city, but a new adventure was calling us. However, we didn't understand the true nature of the journey ahead.

Officer Training School was exactly what I expected. I thrived in that type of leadership training and was named my flight's commander (flight is a term for military units in the Air Force). That basically meant I was the liaison between our flight and the major assigned to us. I enjoyed my time there and even had the honor of my great uncle, who I loved dearly and admired deeply, giving me the first salute at my commissioning ceremony. He had been enlisted in the Air Force back in the 1950's, during the Korean War.

Graduation day came, and I was very proud to march in that parade in front of my family. I drove home with my wife and kids and reported to my unit before the Christmas holiday. Things were going exactly as planned. Alabama even beat Texas to win the National Championship that January. Everything was perfect. Life could not get any better.

CHAPTER FOUR:
First Diagnosis and First Miracle

Our ideal life didn't last very long.

Saturday, January 9th, 2010: After the episode with dizziness described in the introduction, the doctor ordered a CAT scan. We got the results and there was a blank spot on the scan that concerned him. The CAT scan didn't give enough detail to make any definite conclusions, so he admitted me to the hospital and ordered an MRI for Monday morning.

Monday, January 11^{th,} 2010: Warner Robins, Georgia. A doctor stood in the doorway of my hospital room and informed me that I had a brain tumor. He said it was serious. Then he said they were looking for hospitals that could treat me since they did not have the required expertise. That was all he told us.

The news hit me like a sledgehammer to my chest. Casey and I were stunned. By this point, we had been thinking that maybe the symptoms were being caused by a brain aneurysm. My family's medical history included brain aneurysms, but a tumor had never crossed our minds. At that time, the only thing I knew about brain tumors is that they were fatal. My first thought was my family. Our kids were ages 11, 9, 4, and 1 at the time.

We really weren't told much about treatment options. There was no mention of surgery yet. We didn't know the severity of the tumor. Though, it was apparent the situation was dire because we were told I would be transported by ambulance that night to Emory Hospital for further evaluation. Through a series of personal connections and recommendations, I ended up getting referred instead to the Kirkland Clinic of UAB Hospital in Birmingham, Alabama. I was to be transported to Birmingham by ambulance that same night. I called my unit commander to give him the news. I told him I didn't know if or when I would return.

My parents drove to Georgia from Tuscaloosa, Alabama—about a 5-hour trip—to help us with the kids. They knew something was seriously wrong. My dad and Casey followed me in the ambulance to Birmingham while my stepmom, Judy, brought the kids back to their house. A roughly four-hour drive, the ride to Birmingham felt like it took forever. It was just me and my thoughts in the back of that ambulance. I prayed, of course, but I also spent a lot of time trying to figure out exactly what was happening to me and why. We had looked up information about tumors online, so I knew there was a possibility the tumor was benign. That was my primary prayer at that point: "God, please let it be benign."

When we arrived, they insisted I ride on a stretcher even though I felt fine. The nurses were shocked that I was the patient they were waiting for because I looked and acted perfectly healthy. They admitted me to the hospital and put me in a room. When Casey got there, we prayed together about what was in front of us.

Early the next morning the neuro-surgeon, Dr. Barton Guthrie, came into the room and his message was very blunt. He told us the tumor was extremely close to the brain stem and there wasn't time for a biopsy. If he waited and the tumor reached the brain stem, that would make it inoperable. I now consider this to be the first miracle, or divine intervention, in my story—that we found the tumor just in time.

If you recall, I thought I had the stomach flu and just needed to wait it out at home. But Casey was concerned and called an ambulance immediately. Looking back, it would have been easy to think of this as an overreaction to vomiting and dizziness. But her sense of urgent concern was exactly what we needed. If I had waited only one or two more days before going to the hospital, my story might be completely different.

Dr. Guthrie recommended for me to have surgery first thing in the morning on the following day. That afternoon and evening were filled with family and friends visiting me. I didn't know what kind of experience to expect with surgery because I'd never had any kind of surgery. I had never even broken a bone before. I had always been totally healthy. We didn't know what tomorrow held, but we knew that brain surgery had a high level of risk so we visited as long as we could. Casey and I had a sense of peace that night and slept deeply. I knew Jesus would be right there with me during the surgery.

They woke us up crazy early for the surgery. Around 4:30 in the morning, I was taken to a prep room where they shaved my head. I still had hair at that time—I was only 29. I remember this doctor coming in and asking me, "It's on the right side, right?" I confirmed and then he drew an arrow on the back of my head. Everything was happening so fast.

My family would take turns coming to see me in the prep room. When it was just my dad and Casey back there with me, I told my dad, "If this doesn't go well, I'll wake up in the Throne Room of Heaven, but I'll need you to help my wife and kids get through this." I prayed with them, and the nurses wheeled me back. I saw the tumor on a screen for the first time in the operating room. It looked like a golf ball in my head. I remember thinking, "Wow. I can't believe that has been in my head all this time." Soon a nurse was standing over me asking if I was ready, and then I drifted off.

I gradually came around, and I was in a lot of pain. I felt Casey when she entered the room. I don't know how to explain that because I couldn't see her—I couldn't even open my eyes—but I knew she had walked into the room. I called for her. I couldn't lift my head to save my life. Everything was hazy, and the button for the morphine drip was useless. Everything seemed very loud, and my dad incurred my wrath when his cell phone started ringing. The nurse was hearing from me how the drip was not working, and I was frustrated. But I was happy to be alive.

Soon I was in the Neuro ICU and then later on in a regular room. I learned the surgery had lasted 9 hours. They also told me that Dr. Guthrie said everything went well, and that he was able to remove all of the tumor.

Plenty of people were praying because of word of mouth and a relatively new social media platform called Facebook. Our neighbor from Scott AFB put up a "Prayer for Craig Davis" Facebook page to give out updates. It has been maintained, and you can go there today and get a sense of how confusing and rushed those first few days were. You can also get more of a real-time feel for the battles we went through.

Good friends of ours from Tuscaloosa helped with the kids and brought them to see me. We had to go to the waiting room to visit, but I hadn't seen them since the night before the surgery. I was overjoyed to see them and get hugs and kisses.

The worst part of the surgery was my that tongue swelled to the point that I could not swallow food. It stayed like this for five days, and nobody could explain why—other than it could have been the anesthesia or being face down for 9 hours. I survived on fluids and jello with the occasional milkshake. My days consisted of physical therapy and trying to get stronger. The tumor was in the motor skills area of my brain. This was the start of many physical struggles that I still contend with today.

CHAPTER FIVE:
Finding a Church and
Finding Hope

In early February, I finally got to go home to Georgia. By this time a wonderful couple that we barely knew had kind of adopted our family, so the kids didn't miss much school. I got to watch the Saints beat the Colts in the Super Bowl, so my two favorite football teams had won championships in the same year. My commander basically told me to take as much time as I needed away from work. The base medical group assigned a care coordinator to my case, which made getting through the referrals and other Tricare paperwork much easier.

We were still trying to find a church home when I got sick. Trying to find a place that was as amazing as our church back in Illinois was very hard. We hardly knew anybody in the area, and we felt alone. We were desperately searching for the right church to go through this fight with us.

Soon we would be traveling back to Birmingham to meet with the doctors. We had to get the pathology results for the tumor and start determining my treatment options. My mother-in-law worked for an apartment complex in Northport, Alabama, that was gracious enough to let us stay in one of the executive apartments. It was about 45 minutes from the hospital, but it was a major blessing to have a nice, private place to stay while taking care of my medical needs.

We went to the follow-up appointment with Dr. Guthrie to have the stitches removed from my head and to learn whether the tumor was malignant or benign. The stitches came out with no problem. The doctor told me, Casey, and my dad that the tumor was malignant. It was the first time that the tumor had a name: medulloblastoma. He explained that it was typically a pediatric cancer.

Adult cases are rare, but because of the blueish color he observed, Dr. Guthrie was pretty sure he knew the type the day he removed it. He gave me the name of a neuro-oncologist and a follow-up appointment date. With grim faces, he and his assistant told me they were sorry. That was it. I was now officially a cancer patient.

While I had done some research into brain cancer, I now knew the specific name of my cancer. I would even refer to the disease in that way for a long time, as "my cancer" or "my tumor." I still had no idea of what I was facing mentally, physically, and spiritually. At this point I was still naive enough to believe surgery was the toughest part.

We met with the neuro-oncologist soon after and that is when the real fear set in. We started to understand that there was a major battle still ahead of us. Our problem wasn't completely resolved by surgery alone. First, we had to get a brain-spine MRI in order to fully evaluate the results of the surgery. This would also serve as a check to see if there were any other tumors. For this test, I had to spend about 3 hours inside the machine.

Having previously had a couple of brain MRIs, I already knew this was not my favorite activity. The patient must lay perfectly still for a long time in an extremely confined space while the machine makes all kinds of whirling and banging noises— noises which children often compare to jackhammers and rocket ships.[1] All of that together makes for a pretty awful experience. I would learn to use this time to pray. I would try to listen to the Holy Spirit and receive His comfort.

For my next procedure, I had to endure my first lumbar puncture, or spinal tap, to make sure that the cancer cells had not spread to my spine. When you're in this type of situation, you tend to want as much information as you can get. I already had a vague idea of what medulloblastoma was from doing some quick research on Google. But now that I had more time, I was diving in a little more.

Medulloblastoma is generally rare, but is still the most common cancerous brain tumor in children.[2] It is always found in the cerebellum (back of the brain). In adults, there are only about 120 new cases per year in the United States.[3] There is no known cause of the cancer other than the devil at work. Like it says in John 10:10, *"The thief comes only to steal and kill and destroy."* (NIV) I believe that cancer is straight out of Hell and affects young, healthy, and old alike. While researching, I found a movie called *Letters to God* about a young boy with this same disease. The movie totally wrecked me because I realized how much the disease would affect the lives of everyone around me.

Mirek Hufton, the brother of my pastor back in Illinois, had a church just north of Atlanta. I remembered his story about battling cancer and that he had come to our church for healing services. At that time, I was leery of physical healing ministry and wasn't sure what to think of him. After my diagnosis, I decided to go ahead and read his book.

Also, some of our friends from Illinois, Scott and Ranae Wood, had moved to Georgia around the same time as us. They suggested that I go to Roswell one Sunday so that Mirek could lay hands on me and pray for healing. They even offered to drive us, so I accepted their invitation. This time I was in a completely different state of mind regarding healing ministry. His book *Receiving God's Mercy* has continued to inspire me and to build my confidence and hope in God's healing provision for me.

CHAPTER SIX: Starting Medical Treatment

When it came time to start my post-surgery cancer treatments, the doctor recommended 30 sessions of radiation followed by a chemotherapy regime. The good news was that I could receive treatment at a cancer care clinic that was a few miles from my house in Georgia. This would provide less interruption to the kids' lives. Casey and I went back to Warner Robins to take on this next step in the journey.

On my first visit to the clinic, I was fitted for my radiation mask. I grew to hate this mask. My face was swelling from steroids—steroids that I was taking to prevent my brain from swelling. This made my face more sensitive, and the mask was extremely tight. I would leave each radiation session with an imprint on my face. However, the 30 sessions went by quickly without anything significant happening. The real struggle was at home and in my head.

I wasn't used to sitting around doing nothing. We still had not found a church that we could call our new church home. We missed the people at our church back in Illinois, as well as the worship and teaching we received there. The only people we had gotten to know were a few ladies from the gym where Casey was working out, plus that wonderful couple in our neighborhood who would go on to become our life-long friends. The ladies from the gym were amazing and did some wonderful things for us. They cleaned our house while we were away in Birmingham and purchased groceries and supplies for our family. So we weren't totally alone, but in my heart I needed to connect to the body of Christ, and I was crying out to God for direction.

We were already strong believers before the cancer struck, but we had never truly experienced God in such a powerful way as we did during this crisis. Our friends and family were not in Warner Robins, except for the people I mentioned, so we had to come to know God as our total provider. We depended on Him for everything. He was my healer and comforter during times of fear and doubt. If you researched and read about the outcomes of medulloblastoma, you would probably believe there was no hope. But Jesus was with us every step of the journey.

Searching online, I found a church in Macon, Georgia, which was about 45 minutes from our house. I wanted to check it out because their theology was very close to ours and the worship style seemed like what we were used to back home. There was nothing wrong with any of the churches we had visited. We are all one body, the bride of Jesus. But you know when you are in a church home that fits. One of my pastors explained it like this: "Churches are like milkshakes. You can get vanilla, chocolate, or strawberry. They're different, but all made of ice cream (Jesus) and milk (Bible)." To my surprise this church had a campus just a few miles from our house. We had missed it because they had a Spanish sign in the front. There was a Spanish-speaking church which also met there. This new church, Christ Chapel Warner Robins, was an answer to our prayers.

The next Sunday we went to a service there, and it took me about five minutes to know we were in the right place. I could feel His presence in that house immediately. Over the course of our time there, this church and the people in it became an oasis at a very dry time in our lives. I was unable to be as active in the church as I normally would be. But my meetings with Pastor Andy King lifted my spirits. The times I was able to share with some of the other church members about the battle we were going through helped me to process everything. The pastor gave the congregation freedom to share what the Lord was laying on their hearts, and my soul was nourished. We made wonderful friends who we continue to walk through life with even though we are now geographically separated.

Life and treatment kept moving forward. I was incredibly bored and couldn't sleep because of all the medication I was taking. On a whim, my friend Tommy and I decided to take our boys down to Florida to experience spring training. My time in St. Louis had made me an avid Cardinals fan, and Tommy was a Braves fan. We planned out our trip and drove down there while the boys were having their spring break from school. It was an experience I would like to repeat one day. At that time, it broke up the monotony of treatment and helped by injecting some much-needed fun into my world.

Once the radiation was finished, I had a medical port placed in my chest to help with the chemo. The kids were in school, and my commander stayed true to his policy of me taking as much time as I needed to heal. I think by that time he already knew the outcome of my Air Force career, and he didn't want to burden me with unnecessary work. I already missed being part of the unit and putting the skills I learned at OTS to use, but my focus was on my health and surviving the battle.

Chemotherapy proved to be as awful as I had heard it would be. The sessions were spread apart, so I wasn't at the clinic every day like with radiation, but the days were long when I was there. The port did not function correctly, and I would do all kinds of tricks to try and make it work before giving in and getting an IV placed.

CHAPTER SEVEN: New Reality

I can vividly recall the day when my hair fell out in the shower. I went to wash my hair and it just started coming out all over the place. Standing there staring at chunks of hair in my hands, everything became much more real to me. I was no longer the young, healthy Air Force officer. I was a cancer patient. I broke down in tears in the shower. Casey was at the gym. I called her and could barely get out the words about what was happening and why I was crying. When she got home, we finished the job by shaving off what was left of my hair.

Days were long, and I struggled for things to do. At the same time, I struggled with feelings of wanting to withdraw and just do nothing. I purchased the MLB TV package, so I could watch the St. Louis Cardinals and late-night games on the West Coast. I read a lot, including the book *Heaven* by Randy Alcorn. If you've read that book, you know how long it is. I even cleaned up and labeled my emails, which is how I rediscovered the email about my dream from 2008 (the one where Jesus told me I had a tumor). I started to plan the next chapter of my life because it was becoming clear that I would not be in the Air Force.

My primary care doctor on base and my care coordinator told me that my case would be presented at the next medical board. After the board met, I was given a medical retirement date. This was a blessing from God because it would be just like I served a full 20 years, which is the normal retirement threshold. I would get a full retirement check as a Second Lieutenant, my rank after OTS. We would also have base privileges, such as being able to shop at the commissary. That meant we would be able to buy groceries and other household items at a huge discount. Most importantly, our family would be covered by Tricare for life.

Tricare is an insurance program available to active duty military or anyone who is retired from the military. All of my medical expenses for life were now covered thanks to our country's great military and to my heavenly Father. If you recall, I had strongly considered leaving the military only a short time before finding out I had cancer. The reason I didn't leave the Air Force is that I felt like the Lord clearly directed me to go to OTS when I had sought Him for answers back at Line Camp Cabin. God always knows exactly what He's doing.

You can always trust His direction. You cannot go wrong by following Him.

We packed up all the medical records and got an appointment with the Veterans Administration. Normally, the process of determining service-connected disability can be tedious and long, but a recently implemented process sped my case through the bureaucracy. It was quickly determined that I would be given a temporary, 100% VA service-connected disability. This was another huge blessing because it basically meant about $600 more income for us each month. Not only that, but I also would save about $600 per month on my property taxes.

The VA rating would have other benefits as well down the road. God continued to show me how vital the decision made in those Missouri hills had been. At the time of this writing, I estimate that my total medical expenses have been somewhere between $2-3 million, and we've never even seen a bill. While my family has been through a lot of difficulty, we have experienced God's goodness and provision throughout the entire ordeal.

The chief from my old unit, who was now a civilian, told me that there was an opening for a civil service position if we wanted to move back to the St. Louis area. Military bases are full of civil service, private contractor, and other civilian employees. If I took this job, I would be a private citizen working for the Air Force Civilian Services at Scott Air Force Base. We felt like St. Louis was our home now. With the cancer in remission and my Air Force career now over, we knew God was leading us back there. In March of 2011, just a year and a half after coming to Warner Robins, we were loading the van and heading back north.

When we first moved back to Illinois, we took advantage of a program that allowed retirees to rent a house on base. I went through the process of applying for and accepting the civil service position. Soon, I was back in my old flight but this time in civilian clothes instead of uniform. That wasn't the only difference. My physical appearance was drastically different now. My body was swollen from incorrect dosing of steroids and lack of any real exercise. I still could not do things that I used to do, like play golf or go for runs. I wasn't sure if those abilities would ever come back, but I was just glad to be back in our adopted hometown.

It wasn't long before I knew that the civil service job was not for me. I was in a different place physically and mentally the last time I was in the flight, and I felt restricted as far as my day to day tasks. To be blunt, I was outright bored with my daily tasks. We had also picked up a terrible habit of smoking cigarettes again at the end of our time in Warner Robins, so I spent a lot of time being bored and smoking.

I did not want to acknowledge it then, but looking back I believe that I was suffering from depression. I lived in constant fear of the cancer coming back, and I was still having MRI exams done on my brain every 3 months. The anticipation of getting the MRI results always added to my fear. The tests made it impossible to forget about the reality that the cancer could come back. I was still mourning the loss of my old life—the life I had before cancer. It did not help to be living on base, working daily in my old unit, and seeing my co-workers still in uniform. There were just too many memories for me to overcome.

I thought the solution might be to change jobs and work in a different location on base. It's rare for someone to give up the security of a government service job for one with a contractor, but I felt like I needed the change. I started work for Booz Allen in November of 2011. Eventually, I was transferred to a team which included some of my friends from past work. I believed this was going to last a while, so I started feeling optimistic again.

CHAPTER EIGHT: Life Without Cancer and My Miracle Boys

Meanwhile, we decided to move off base and buy another home. Casey and I were searching online and trying to find the right house to settle into and raise our family. After looking at what felt like a million houses, we found one in O'Fallon which fit us perfectly. We moved in January of 2012. It was bigger than any house I had ever lived in, and we were ecstatic. We were in a good neighborhood that was central to St. Louis and the base. We also had access to great schools for the kids.

Casey and I did not feel like our family was complete. We wanted another baby and we were praying about it from the time we moved back. After many months of trying, I asked my endocrinologist at Siteman what the possibilities were for us to have a baby. He said I was not going to be able to produce enough hormones due to my adrenal gland receiving damage from the prior radiation and chemotherapy. For that reason, he informed us that having a baby was not possible. Casey had been praying diligently for 14 months, asking God for yet another miracle. Our family got a late Christmas present, and we found out we were expecting a baby. God proved the doctor wrong, and in August of 2013, we welcomed Jaxson to our family. My wife may have been a little bit excited:

https://www.facebook.com/craig.davis.501/posts/472669099435871

The contract I was working on for Booz Allen was about to expire, and a different company had won the bidding for a new IT support contract with the Air Force. We had the option to simply change badges and continue to do the same work for a new company, but I decided to see what the civilian world had to offer instead. I believed I needed to get a job away from the Air Force to be able to reach my full potential.

Not long before Jaxson was born, I found a great opportunity with a Catholic health management organization. They had a motto about revealing the healing presence of God. The situation felt perfect. It seemed to have everything I was looking for, so I accepted the job. Sisters of Saint Mary (SSM) Health was great for my growth as a SharePoint developer, and I learned a lot of new skills. They had a flexible work from home policy, which met my needs perfectly. There was even time for me to obtain my MBA at Fontbonne University, which was right down the road from my office. I had goals of moving up in management. A few of the projects I was working on were going great, which would certainly help me achieve my goal of being promoted.

Life was moving along at home. We had two teenagers, two young girls, and a rambunctious toddler at home. Between their school work, my school work, my job, and our church life, we were very busy. I was finally able to buy my dream truck: a brand new, red, 4X4 Ford F150. We went on vacations to the beach, exercised regularly, and enjoyed life. God even extended our family again. We added little Owen in September of 2015. God had answered our prayers with not just one, but two miracle boys. Once again, everything had fallen into place. Life seemed about as close to perfect as it could get.

CHAPTER NINE:
Devastating News

With our lives running at a fast pace, Casey and I decided to schedule a time for us to get away without the kids. I found a beautiful bed & breakfast right off of the beach in Destin, Florida, which was couples only. It looked to be very romantic and peaceful. The cost was high, but I thought it would be worth it. We booked it for the coming July (2016). My next MRI wasn't until September, as I had just been scheduled for annual MRIs instead of semi-annual. At that time, I was feeling great physically.

Over the next few months things started to happen that made the old fears and worries come back. My left arm was weaker than my right, and I was starting to have dizzy spells after sitting up quickly. I called my neuro-oncologist at Siteman to see if we could move the MRI appointment forward. I wanted to get it done before the trip. I felt like I needed to know if something was happening or if it was my active imagination.

I had an hour to think while lying in the MRI machine. My mind was mostly fixed on what was about to happen if the results were not good. We walked into the back of Dr. Campian's office on the 7th floor of the Siteman Center in St. Louis. We had done this a dozen times over the previous six and a half years. But this time, I knew in my heart it was different. Dr. Campian was already in the room instead of her nurse, which was unusual. I knew she was there to deliver bad news.

Slowly, she started shaking her head in disappointment. She explained to us that the cancer had returned, and it was not good. This time the tumor had returned in a different location and surgery was almost certainly not an option. All of my fears were proving to be true. I was devasted and heartbroken. I started blurting out questions. "Are you sure it's not surgical?"

"What do you mean you are not sure of my options?"

It felt lonely—like God had abandoned me. I was supposed to be healed already. Everything was going great again. We had been blessed with two new sons, a few great jobs, and a nice house since the last battle. I thought we were through with cancer and that it was defeated. Casey seemed to be in shock. I had to go to the bathroom and collect myself.

You can see from these Facebook posts, and others we made over those first few days, how much shock we were in:

Casey Davis
July 18, 2016 · O'Fallon, IL · 🌐

···

We are entering a season we hoped we would never be in again and yet we are here...

We got the news today Craig's brain cancer is back. This time it is really close to the brain stem so they are not sure if surgery is possible.

I would like to ask for you to agree in prayer for two things as we wait to see what his treatment is going to look like.

1) That surgery will be possible and very successful with a total removal of the tumor.

2) That it has not spread. (He has another MRI next week of the spine)

We are trusting God. He has been faithful in the past and he will continue to be faithful in the future! Thank you in advance for standing with us.

 DJ-Melinda McKinney and 49 others   107 Comments 30 Shares

https://www.facebook.com/story.php?story_fbid=10206906431554852&id=1099603441

 Prayer for Craig Davis
July 20, 2016 · O'Fallon, IL · 🌐

···

Update on Craig....... We found out that the tumor is inoperable. At this point he has a few test he has to get done to make sure it hasn't spread and we also have an appointment set up with a Radiation therapist to see what our options are there. We meet with his oncologist on August 1 to review the results and come up with a game plan. We know that this report is not a good one, but we also know that God is bigger and that he is in control in this situation. Please continue to be in prayer over the next few weeks as we try to find the best and most effective treatment plan for Craig. I don't believe God is finished with him yet! I believe he still has MANY years ahead of him! Thank you all for praying with me

 13   12 Comments 1 Share

https://www.facebook.com/permalink.php?story_fbid=10153796687291245&id=251782711244

It was hard news to accept and even harder to tell our friends and family. I had to call my dad on

46

his birthday, July 18th, and give him this awful news. I called my mom and my brother, Brad, to explain the situation to them. My head was swimming with thoughts as I was already planning to investigate the latest research, clinical trials, and medical advancements since 2010. The fact that this time was different—and much more dangerous—hadn't sunk in yet.

We went home and planned how we were going to tell the kids and our friends the terrible news. The doctor told us to go ahead and go on the vacation we had planned. I could tell by her demeanor and the way she was talking to me that she thought I had no chance of surviving this tumor. We decided to tell the kids after the trip to Destin in order to give us time to process everything. The plan was to leave in a few days. I had a co-worker who was connected to the neurological unit at Vanderbilt University Hospital. She was able to get me an appointment for a second opinion as to whether the tumor was surgical or not. The appointment was scheduled for the day after we would return from Destin.

Before leaving for the trip, we gathered at our close friends Scott and Ranae Wood's house. Eric and Juliana Staub were there along with another couple. They wanted to pray with us and give us room to talk out our feelings. At that time, I was hesitant to declare that I was going to be healed. I was afraid that if I declared healing and then the Lord decided to call me home, I would be hurting the faith of my friends and family. I feared I would especially be harming those not close to God by inhibiting their ability to trust Him. I certainly didn't want to cause anyone to blame God for my death. Eric challenged that belief because he was convinced I was going to be healed. He said that it is God's desire to heal everyone and pointed out that Jesus never refused to heal anyone in the gospels.

God's family operates as a body. That's why it's so important and such a huge blessing to have other believers walking closely with us through hard times. They will have faith during those moments when we have doubts. We fill in each other's gaps and help each other. James 5:16 tells us, *"Confess your sins to each other and pray for each other so that you may be healed. The earnest prayer of a righteous person has great power and produces wonderful results."* (NLT) I cannot put into words how much my Christian family helped during these dark times. If you don't know Jesus, please consider Him. Only He can bring peace and salvation into your life and make you part of God's family.

Eric's daughter sang a worship song for us that I had never heard before. It was called "Take Courage" by Kristene DiMarco. The song became prophetic over my circumstance. It encouraged us to be strong during the struggle because God is with us. He's with us in the midst of waiting for our situations to change. And if we're looking for a miracle to happen, we only need to keep our eyes fixed on Jesus. The song became a battle cry for us. But I still wanted to honor God and not "test Him" by guaranteeing my healing publicly.

The pastors from our church heard about the situation we were facing. We had been in Georgia during the first battle, but they were aware of my history and knew that any recurrence was bad news—especially an inoperable tumor. In James 5:14, the Bible says, *"Is anyone among you sick? Let them call the elders of the church to pray over them and anoint them with oil in the name of the Lord."* (NIV) My pastors came to my house and anointed me with oil and prayed for me to be healed. I was still speaking of not "testing God." Pastor Rick understood where I was coming from. I wanted to let God be God. I wanted to honor Him and His will.

CHAPTER TEN: Destin's Beaches and God's Promises

We dropped the kids off at our friends' place and went to the airport for the trip. Our minds were burdened, but at this time I was still physically able to do pretty much everything without restriction. When we got to Henderson Inn, we were blown away by its beauty. Located next to Henderson State Park, with no high-rise condos in view, it had a tranquility about it. It had about 30 rooms in two separate buildings, and the facility is adults only. It's also relatively small, so it's generally a quiet place. We felt a strong sense of peace there and knew that this was the place for us to deal with God about the diagnosis.

The first phase was to mourn the life we had built over the past 6 ½ years. Having gone through the previous battle, we understood that our daily lives were about to change significantly. I had to let go of the job I loved and the activities we had grown accustomed to as a family because we knew that this fight was going to take everything we had. I was mourning in a different way as well. I was convinced that I might not survive this battle. I still didn't know for sure whether there would be any surgery or radiation, but I knew from my experience with chemotherapy that the battle would require me to fight mentally, physically, and emotionally. To be honest, I didn't know how much I really wanted to fight. Even if I wanted to, I wasn't sure how much fight I had left in me.

I was honest with Casey and God as we sat on Destin's sandy shores. My wife, kids, and extended family were heavy on my heart. Owen had not yet turned one and Jaxson was almost three. I was now angry at God for blessing us with these two miracle boys because, in my mind, I wasn't going to get to see them grow up. I was worried about Casey and the kids being able to support themselves since I was the primary breadwinner in our family and took care of all the financial responsibilities. I knew that another man would eventually need to fill my role as her husband and the kids' father figure. I was intensely jealous of this man, but at the same time I was praying for him to be the right man for my family. My heart broke over and over as I thought about leaving them.

We floated in the gorgeous ocean waters of the Gulf of Mexico and talked about these deep issues—all the while bawling our eyes out and reaching to God for answers. Our souls were laid bare on those beaches for the next three days. The Holy Spirit ministered to us, and it felt like Jesus was right there beside us. Down in the pit of our souls, we were being fed promises from God's Word that would strengthen us for the months ahead. Jeremiah 29:11-12 spoke to us deeply, saying, *"'For I know the plans I have for you,' declares the Lord, 'plans to prosper you and not to harm you, plans to give you hope and a future. Then you will call on me and come and pray to me, and I will listen to you.'"* (NIV) These promises would give us confidence in the Lord during the toughest times, no matter the news we were receiving.

On the last day, a beautiful rainbow appeared as if to seal the word we had received. As you can see from this Facebook post, we viewed it as a reminder to trust God's promises:

Casey Davis is with Craig Davis at Henderson Park Inn.
July 23, 2016 · Destin, FL · 🌐

God gave us a beautiful rainbow this morning to look at while we drank our coffee. He was reminding us to trust his promises.

https://www.facebook.com/story.php?story_fbid=10206938146267700&id=1099603441

We flew home and then drove down to Nashville to get the second opinion on surgical options. We still held out hope that the tumor could be removed since that was our only experience with cancer up to this point. My dad met us there. We had breakfast and talked about our hopes for the appointment. It did not take long after reviewing the MRI images for this highly confident neurosurgeon and his team to come into the room. He said he would often cut into places that others would not, but there was no way to cut into the location of my tumor. We did not understand what we had seen up to this point. We did not realize until now that the tumor was actually inside my brain stem.

We picked up the two oldest kids in Kentucky on our way home from Nashville. They stayed there visiting Casey's family while we were out of town. On the ride home, we gave them the details as we knew them. We had already told them about the cancer returning, but now we also told them the tumor was inoperable. There were a lot of tears. They were both old enough to remember the battle in 2010. They knew how hard it was, and the fact that this time would be even more challenging made it harder to swallow. I was thinking that I might not get to walk my daughters down the aisle at their weddings or to see my sons grow into manhood. I was realizing that I might not be there to give them fatherly advice for life's challenges, and it hurt deeply. You can get some sense of the hurt I was feeling in this Facebook post:

Prayer for Craig Davis
July 25, 2016 · Massac, KY · 🌐   •••

This update was written by Craig.....

The visit today at Vanderbilt did not result in immediate treatment options. The tumor is inoperable and proton therapy might be difficult due to my previous radiation. The hope we were given is that there could be some new drugs that have shown the potential to reduce or eliminate the tumor if my subtype of Medulloblastoma matches the subtypes where they have been effective. We will just be dependent on my previous tumors pathology and guess that they are a match.

I am not saying that there is no hope. Our hope comes from the Lord and I trust Gods plan for my life and my family. This is not where we belong as believers in Jesus Christ. We believe he was resurrected and that our eternity is secure in heaven thru his blood bought righteousness and forgiveness.

I ask you if you were in my position where will your mind be. Its easy to dismiss God and his authority on your life. I've definitely made my share of mistakes but each one of us will come to the end of life. For me, I know that I will be wrapped in Gods embrace.

I ask that you all be in prayer for a miracle for the Lord. It hurts my heart so much to leave my family behind and miss all the moments thats in front of them. Please pray for their comfort and peace. I will never be able to thank everyone enough for the love thats been shown to my family. They are my heartbeat.

If you don't know Jesus as your saviour I ask that you consider him. Forget all the rules and the religion. He is the only one that can give you peace, both in the battle I am facing and in your life. I would love to see you all with me in heaven. Be sure of your beliefs and your faith because one day you will be in my position or death could happen suddenly. Don't let a day go by without Jesus in your life.

Don't think I am giving up. I'll fight to my final breath.

To God be the Glory

Craig

👍❤️😢 83   45 Comments 44 Shares

When we got home, we gave the other four kids the rundown of what was going to happen regarding my treatment. The girls were alive for the 2010 initial diagnosis, but they really didn't remember anything. Our youngest boys were not yet born in 2010. Even now, they were too young to really grasp what was happening. Casey and I explained that there would be a lot of appointments and Daddy would be sick. We prayed with them and said that Daddy would need a lot of prayer, which Jaxson took seriously. He would pray for me every chance he got, and his prayers would often move me to tears because of how simple they were and how completely he believed Jesus would heal me. I believe God was working through his faith. Maybe God had given me Jaxson at just the right time.

CHAPTER ELEVEN: Treatment, Again

We looked into the possibility of a biopsy. There was concern that the tumor could be a different type of cancer because it had recurred in a different spot than its original location. There would also be a benefit to knowing the tumor's pathology. There was a drug that was working in prolonging life for some patients with a specific subtype of medulloblastoma. The subtypes and the drug were new developments that were not around in 2010, and a biopsy could tell us if my tumor was this subtype. Unfortunately, a consult with the neurosurgeon ruled out a biopsy due to the risk of paralysis. The team at Siteman gave me my options for treatment.

Their recommended course of action would be proton radiation therapy followed by three cycles of chemotherapy. The radiation oncologist, Dr. Huang, had determined that I could receive a limited dose of proton radiation, which was different from traditional radiation. It is more concentrated and affects a smaller area around its target. There is only a certain amount of radiation the brain can handle before experiencing adverse effects. However, due to the location of the tumor, he felt proton radiation treatment would be safe.

Around August 9th, I woke up in the middle of the night to go to the bathroom. When I went to stand up, my left leg completely gave out from under me, and I fell to the floor. As I was lying there, I realized that I couldn't move my left arm or hand, including my fingers. Deep fear swept over me as Casey was asking what was wrong. The world seemed to be crashing down as I began to understand how quickly this tumor was progressing and starting to affect me physically. I had read about how the brain stem is the conduit for breathing, swallowing, and other vital bodily functions. All signals go through the brain stem. During just a few hours of sleep, the tumor had grown to the point that it had cut off my left side completely. This night was my lowest point emotionally. I felt strongly that my time here on earth was coming to an end. Casey and I prayed and cried together the rest of the night.

A few days later my dad drove up from Tuscaloosa to stay with us for a few weeks. He wanted to spend time with us while helping to do some modifications to our home. I could no longer go up the stairs to our bedroom. Casey moved our bed downstairs to a room that doubled as my office and a playroom for the kids. My friend, Eric, was home from the mission field by God's grace. I needed him to be here for me, and Casey needed his wife, Juliana, just as much. My dad and Eric installed doors on our new bedroom and converted the closet into a bathroom. I now could live just on the main floor of our home. This kind of constant help meant a lot to us. We were always facing new challenges, but we weren't facing any of them alone:

Casey Davis is with Craig Davis and 2 others.
August 9, 2016 · 🌐   •••

Blessed to have friends and family working so hard to make our house more accessible for Craig. They are tearing out closets and putting in a shower on the main level. We are also turning our office on the main level into our bedroom. We couldn't be doing these things without the help of our friends and family!

Continue to pray for Craig. He had his radiation planning session yesterday and his radiation oncologist wants him to start asap. So as soon as the plan is ready they will call us and he will start. Thank you all for your many prayers for Craig and our family. We truly appreciate them.

https://www.facebook.com/story.php?story_fbid=10207059482301025&id=1099603441

Dad had been there for me during the first battle with cancer, but it was different that first time. He was building a new home and was doing a lot of the work himself and overseeing the rest. Also, he and my stepmom, Judy, had recently taken custody of my two nieces. It was obvious Dad had a lot going on during this period, but I still let his absence hurt me at times. I believe now that the Holy Spirit was teaching me to have total reliance on my Father in Heaven.

This time, I would not be able to count the number of miles Dad put on his vehicles driving from Tuscaloosa to our home here in O'Fallon, Illinois. He was here with us as often as possible to help around the house, be with me at treatments, and just spend precious time with us. As a result, we have grown closer than at any other point in my life.

As strange as it is to say, there are benefits to going through something like cancer. Cancer is a product of sin's curse on the earth. There was no cancer in the world as God created it. He created a perfect world and man introduced sin into that world. God is never the source of anything evil or harmful. But, He can and does bring good from evil and harmful situations. He is always good and never wastes an opportunity. The Bible tells us in Romans 8:28 that *"God causes everything to work together for the good of those who love God."* (NLT) I trusted Him and was seeing how, even in my circumstances, God was bringing good things in my life. Here's how I said it back in 2017:

 Craig Davis updated his status. •••
January 19, 2017 · 🌐

Yesterday was 6 months since we learned the cancer has returned. I remember thinking in those days right after the diagnosis that it would be easier to die suddenly rather than go thru months of pain and a long goodbye. It probably is not possible for me to have been more wrong. Each moment with my wife Casey Davis and kids is precious and I wouldn't want to miss one second. I wouldn't have been able to spend this time with my Dad and family growing closer. I would not have experienced the amazing support and outpouring of love from our friends, church family, and my coworkers. Most of all I wouldn't have had all the time with my Lord and my faith growing in His loving embrace.
Life is precious and a lot of times we take the small moments for granted. Enjoy each breath that the Lord gives you and treasure the small moments. A wise man once said "If you laugh, think, and cry then it was a good day." Live the life God gave you to the fullest.

 126   32 Comments 6 Shares

https://www.facebook.com/craig.davis.501/posts/10211603081009570

My mom also visited during this time. She had some tragedies and bad relationships happen over the previous few years. She was living near my brother, Brad, and his family in Shreveport, Louisiana. Throughout this journey, she has grown closer to God. She eventually moved back closer to some of her family in Deatsville, Alabama. During her visit, she took care of other needs around the house that I couldn't attend to. Mom also did what she loves to do most—cook for us.

CHAPTER TWELVE:
Proton Radiation and Biopsy

Proton therapy is similar to traditional radiation in that you wear a custom fitted mask. However, the machine is different. It's located directly beneath the parking deck of the facility where I was being treated. God's hand had clearly been at work yet again when He led us back to St. Louis. The Siteman Center was one of the very few locations in the United States that had proton therapy available at the time. Proton therapy had only become widely accepted by the medical community in the mid-2000's. Siteman also happens to be a world-class cancer treatment center overall, and it was only 30 minutes from our house. God was always planning ahead for us.

I began the proton therapy the following week after my fall. I believe the date was August the 18th. Dr. Huang wanted to get the tumor under control since it was already beginning to dramatically affect my ability to function. This time the mask was not as much of a problem, and the sessions went quickly. The staff members in the proton center were always incredibly courteous and helpful in getting me onto the machine bed and also getting me situated correctly. They even set my phone up in the room to record a video so that I could see how the machine moved all around me to get the correct areas treated. They were always going the extra mile for me.

After another consult with the neurosurgeon, Dr. Kim, it was determined that the biopsy could go ahead and proceed. Learning more about the pathology was very important. Even though there was the potential for fatality, it was considered unlikely. Paralysis was considered the most significant risk, but I was already partially paralyzed. So, all things considered, it was deemed to be worth the risk. The biopsy was scheduled for the last week of August 2016. My mom was already here, and my dad and Judy would drive up to be here for us before and after the procedure.

After being admitted, but before the procedure, I began to be able to move my fingers on my left hand. This was evidence that the tumor had shrunk a little, and this small improvement gave me hope that the medical procedures were working. A small blood clot was also found in my left calf muscle. The doctors debated on moving forward with the biopsy. A blood doctor determined there was minimal risk, so the biopsy went ahead as planned.

I woke up being carried to a CAT scan machine to see if there was an internal blockage. I was not responding to stimuli, so the doctors were concerned about the possibility I had been paralyzed from the procedure. I remember asking one of the surgeons if the tumor was a blueish-green color, which I knew was the color of medulloblastoma from my first surgeon. The surgeon indicated that the tumor was blueish-green. I began getting some feeling back in my left side while we waited for the pathology results. Those would tell us whether the tumor was the subtype which had showed a response to the trial medication. The results came back and, unfortunately, my tumor was not the correct subtype. It was another crushing blow.

I went home after a day in the neuro ICU and a few days in the main neuro unit. From the start of this battle all the way through today, I have not had a single bad nurse. They have all been thoughtful and kind. Having gone through this, I now have more appreciation for nurses. I view nursing as a very noble profession. They do not make nearly enough money considering the amount of work they do for a lot of hurting, demanding patients. Casey and I viewed them all as our mission field during my stays at the hospital. We tried to have an impact on their spiritual lives as much as they were having an impact on my physical life.

My stay at home did not last long. Complications from the blood clot soon landed me back at the hospital. The clot had moved up my leg, gotten bigger, and become very painful. Ironically, during a late-night CAT scan to get pictures of the clot, the tech dropped me while moving me from the CT table to my stretcher. The drop caused me to sprain my knee. We didn't realize the extent of the injury until I had a terribly painful procedure to drain fluid from my knee. At that point, the doctors determined it had been sprained during the fall. I also got a few extra days in the hospital. It seemed my suffering had no end, as I only had a tiny little TV on which to watch Alabama beat Ole Miss. While I was there, I continued with the proton therapy and had an IVC filter placed in my chest to catch any blood clots before they got to my lungs.

It felt like everything was happening very quickly. I was in the hospital that year for Jaxson, Tristen, Gabby, and Juliana's birthdays. I had used up my paid leave from work and was now on long-term disability. Due to my health history, I had opted for the long-term disability policy when hiring on with SSM Health. It was available to all employees without any kind of underwriting. God had been looking out for us yet again. I also still had my military retirement. I praise God all the time for the decision to go to OTS because it has kept us afloat financially.

CHAPTER THIRTEEN:
Chemotherapy and My Second 2nd Opinion

I finally finished proton therapy. The next step was to have a port placed for the collection of my stem cells and for chemotherapy. The stem cells had to be collected before chemo treatment. While it completely exhausted me, I was thankful that it took only one day to harvest all of the healthy cells I would need for a stem cell transplant:

Prayer for Craig Davis
November 1, 2016 · O'Fallon, IL · 🌐

Praise Report!!! Craig's goal was to collect 5 million stem cells over the next 4 days. Our God showed out and 14.8 million were collected today on the first day! Praise the Lord because the procedure made Craig really weak and tired. God's got this!! All our trust is in Him! Now Craig can rest this week as chemotherapy begins Monday. To God be the Glory! Thank you all who have been praying!

👍❤️😮 200   47 Comments 20 Shares

https://www.facebook.com/permalink.php?story_fbid=10154060199851245&id=251782711244

An oncologist has since confirmed that this was an incredible result.

A week or so prior to getting the good news of this amazing stem cell harvest, I had gone through a struggle with disappointment. We had been praying about the treatment plan my doctor at Siteman gave us. The existing plan just used basic chemo drugs and didn't include anything that was specific to my disease. We started thinking that there had to be something better available than the dreary, standard plan we had been given.

After some research, I found that one of the very few adult medulloblastoma specialists in the United States was at Vanderbilt. I wanted to get a second opinion since most of the available information was based on pediatric cases. Because I had already been a patient there for the second opinion regarding surgical options, it was not hard to get an appointment with Dr. Moots. I had high hopes that he would have some thoughts on how to beat this disease using different medicines and treatment options. I was just looking for hope from a medical doctor. We sent him my records and MRI scans. Dad drove up to Nashville from Tuscaloosa.

When we got into the exam room, my hope came crashing down again. He said basically the same thing that my other doctors had said. He told us that the only hope we had was for the existing treatment plan to buy me a few extra months of life. I was devastated and thought my earthly life would soon be ending. Dying from a brain tumor is never pretty.

After this second opinion, I was frustrated and reeling from the disappointment. Fortunately, even when my faith was weak, there were still other people believing God for me:

 Prayer for Craig Davis updated their status. •••
October 26, 2016 · O'Fallon, IL · 🌐

The visit today with the doctor at Vanderbilt resulted in him recommending the same path as Craig's current oncologist. Starting Friday he will begin the stem cell harvesting process. This will involve getting growth factor shots and long days drawing out the stem cells as I outlined in the previous post.

He will also go ahead and get a MRI done on Oct. 31st that will be used to compare the tumor to both prior to radiation and after two cycles of chemotherapy that he will begin on Nov 7th. If the tumor shows response (shrinking) after two rounds of chemo Craig will receive the high dose of chemo and the stem cell transplant. The group 3/4 subtypes have not typically been chemo responsive, but we serve a mighty God who will be glorified thru this storm and nothing is impossible for Him.

Please pray for the following:
1. He has enough healthy stem cells to harvest.
2. The procedures do not produce any side effects.
3. The chemo medicines being used causes the tumor to respond.
4. Most of all for God to perform a miracle and supernaturally heal Craig and for the tumor to disappear in Jesus name.

 You, Clay Hahn, Jacob Davis and 64 others   42 Comments 17 Shares

https://www.facebook.com/permalink.php?story_fbid=10154044848996245&id=251782711244

I don't know what the stem cell harvest would have been like if it had not been for all of my prayer warriors out there, but I know that God works through the prayers of His people.

CHAPTER FOURTEEN: Building Godly Hope

Hope, from a natural standpoint, is when you have an optimistic *desire* that something is going to happen. Maybe it will come to pass. Maybe it won't, but you are hopeful that it will. Godly hope is having the optimistic *assurance* that something is going to happen. You want it to come to pass, and you believe there is an all-powerful God who also wants the same thing.

Romans 5:5 says, *"Now hope does not disappoint, because the love of God has been poured out in our hearts by the Holy Spirit who was given to us."* (NKJV) I believe hope is a backbone to faith itself because you might not have complete faith yet, but your hope is in God. If you believe He always wants what is best for you, then this hope changes your perspective. It builds faith through trust in who God is—His nature and character. He is perfectly good. He loves you fully. He also happens to be all-powerful. That's quite a combination if you really think about it.

We went back home, and I dug deeper into the Word of God. The Holy Spirit reminded me daily of my dependence on Him. I need Him for every breath I breathe, every single day of my life. That was true before I got cancer, but now I was keeping this perspective all the time. I was speaking healing over my body every day before, but now I was speaking more vigorously and with more conviction. I was reminded of the promises I believed we had received. I thought about the words that had been spoken over me by our friends while they prayed for me.

There were still nights when I couldn't sleep because of worry. Sometimes, the fear of dying would overwhelm me. There were also nights when I would hear the Holy Spirit, or the voice of God, giving me encouragement and reminding me that I was His child. He was comforting me in my tears. It felt like He was right there with me, wiping my tears. I would often roll over during these times so that I could avoid waking Casey up. Many tears were shared between just me and the Lord.

Chemotherapy began that November (2016) before Thanksgiving. Before each drug would start running through my body, I would have Casey lay her hands on the bag of medicine. I would ask God to use the medicine for good and that I would not suffer from the side effects. I would ask the Holy Spirit to use the drugs to complete their intended purpose without causing damage. Here is a Facebook post describing our mindset at the time:

Craig Davis is with Casey Davis.
November 15, 2016 · 🌐

Yesterday was my first day of chemo and with the issues with my port and past experience with the drugs I had a little trepidation over the weekend. As we were settling into the pod where I would get my first round I felt God's peace in my spirit. Even though the regimen was changed unexpectedly and knowing that the treatment is usually not effective on my type tumor I knew He was with me and I was secure in him. There is no replacement for that blessed assurance. That he is mine and I am his and he will be with me.

I will latch onto his promises and hold tight to those truths. As Casey and I laid hands on the chemo bags and prayed over the medicines effectiveness I was overcome with peace that surpasses understanding. The side effects will be minimal to none and these medicines will eliminate what is remaining in Jesus name. To God be the Glory.

Peace I leave with you; my peace I give you. I do not give to you as the world gives. Do not let your hearts be troubled and do not be afraid.
John 14:27 NIV

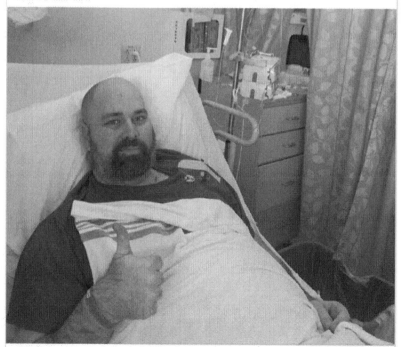

👍❤️ 243   77 Comments 20 Shares

At this point, I was completely depending on God for every aspect of my healing. Some might say, "If you were *completely* depending on Him for your healing, then you shouldn't have received medical treatment." I believe decisions regarding medical treatment, such as which treatments to pursue and how much, are up to each individual. Everyone has to speak to doctors and experts and prayerfully consider their options while ultimately being guided by God's peace. The Bible teaches that every good thing comes from the Lord. So, medicine itself is a gift from God. I believe God uses medical treatments for good and it is only through His gifts to brilliant individuals that these options exist. Refusing medicine in my situation would have been like refusing food and then asking God to keep me from starving to death.

I can only speak for myself, but I feel like Jesus is with me every minute of every day in whatever I may be doing at that time. I believe He uses medical treatments *and* supernatural miracles to achieve His purposes. In all the accounts of Jesus' miracle healings in the Bible, the healing never happens the same way twice. There is no formula for healing. If there were, then it would remove the need for us to have an intimate relationship with

Him. I believe that as we listen to the Holy Spirit speaking into our lives, we get direction for life and for our health. I felt previously and at this point, that receiving medical treatment was a course I should take.

Medical treatments, especially cancer treatments, have their downside. Back in 2010, I developed severe tinnitus during my chemo treatments and lost most of the hearing in my right ear. In 2014, I had an infection of the saliva gland which resulted in total hearing loss for my right ear. I went as far as to take part in a clinical trial at Washington University to have a cochlear implant inserted behind my ear. I could not have one with a magnet due to frequent MRIs, but they have some without magnets. I made the decision not to use it after many hours in a sound booth trying to marry the electronic sounds from my right ear with the natural sounds from my left ear. Also, because there was no magnet on the device, I had to use toupee tape to keep my earpiece attached. That was very difficult, so everything considered, I decided it was not worth the trouble.

Knowing what we had gone through the first time, we were more intentional in praying against the side effects of radiation and chemotherapy treatments this time. God answered and prevented normal complications such as severe nausea, mouth sores, and fatigue. I was even able to enjoy my two favorite holidays—Thanksgiving and Christmas—with my family during the treatments. Here's a Facebook post I wrote that year about some of the things I was thankful for:

Craig Davis updated his status.

November 17, 2016 · 🌐

···

I didn't do the daily thanks for things in my life and chose to combine it all into one post.

First, I am thankful for a God who loves me and gave me the opportunity to have Jesus and the Holy Spirit in my life. Without Him I would be a lost vessel on the rough sea of life without any idea of where I am going and who I am. His saving grace has given me the trust of his purpose for me and the confidence of eternity. Above all else my unshakeable faith in the Lord is the thing I am most thankful for.

The almost twenty years that I have had with Casey is easily next on my thankful list. She is the most wonderful, sweet Christ loving woman and I was blessed beyond measure to have her in my life at such a young age. She is exactly what God had in mind when he created someone for me to share life with during my time here. I love her to the depths of my soul.

She has also blessed me with six children that I am able to pour into. They each have their own personalities and purpose in life. I pray that each of them hear God's voice at a young age and follow his will for their life. I am grateful to have had the opportunity to be their father.

The family and circumstances where you are born also influence so much in the direction of life. God placed me in a loving home with parents and siblings that made me into the man that I am today. In each of their own unique ways they displayed how to love others. Through the battles that I am facing they are there in any way we need them and I am very grateful for that and the time I have with them.

My church family and my friends are the best a guy can wish for in life. I've made unshakable, eternal friendships at FFC that cannot be replaced. I've also had the honor of working with great people the years in the Air Force and other jobs that have become life long friends. I have neighbors who have practically adopted my family during this season. It's humbling and uplifting.

I am a man blessed in ways I cannot express and couldn't hope to get the words right. I love you all and pray that you are blessed this holiday season like never before and you are also overwhelmed with thankfulness.

I will give thanks to you, Lord , with all my heart; I will tell of all your wonderful deeds.
Psalm 9:1 NIV

👍❤ Heather McDaniel Speed, Clay Hahn and 40 others   5 Comments 5 Shares

I would go about every two weeks for a chemo session at Siteman Cancer Center. Each session lasted 4-8 hours depending on the medicine being administered that day. I cannot express how grateful we are to our friends in the area that have always stepped up to provide meals and watch the kids while I was at the hospital. God placed a Christian family to live directly behind us for this season in our lives. Ever since the day of my second diagnosis, this neighbor has cut my grass. And despite having eight kids of their own, they have welcomed my children anytime, day or night. Galatians 5:14 says, *"For all the law is fulfilled in one word, even in this: 'You shall love your neighbor as yourself.'"* (NKJV) They took this verse literally. So did many other people, even though they didn't live next to us. Things would have been much more difficult without all of these wonderful people helping us out.

My Heavenly Father is a loving, gentle, caring Father and it is wonderful to be in His family. The bond between Christian brothers and sisters who walk through life together is indescribably sweet. But it wasn't only Christians who pitched in and did nice things for us. Our entire community made certain that Christmas was especially memorable for our children.

CHAPTER FIFTEEN:
Something We Could See at Just the Right Time

The Christian walk is one of faith. According to Hebrews 11:1, *"Faith is confidence in what we hope for and assurance about what we do not see."* (NIV) As I mentioned in the previous chapter, God allowed us plenty of time and space to believe in what we could not see. He developed godly hope and godly assurance in us. We were believing for complete healing, which was supposed to be impossible. There was certainly no evidence for it much of the time. There was no natural reason to believe I was going to come out of this battle healed and restored. But sometimes God, in His mercy, will give us something that we can see— some evidence that He is listening, answering, and working on our behalf—at just the right time to keep us going and build our confidence.

You can sense from these Facebook posts how God used that kind of evidence and good news to lift our spirits when we desperately needed encouragement:

Prayer for Craig Davis
November 8, 2016 · O'Fallon, IL · 🌐

First we want to give Praise to the Lord that the proton therapy shrunk the tumor significantly. We would have to do the math to give an exact percentage, but we can tell from the MRI images that it was at least 50%.

This is the desired result of the radiation and we are praying for the chemotherapy to eliminate what is remaining. Without further treatments the tumor will begin to grow back quickly. Another image we saw today shows that the tumor is not just on top of the brain stem, but inside it so no amount of shrinkage would make it surgically removeable.

The port that was implanted last Monday appeared to have some possible surface level infection that checked out to be clear. This caused a one week delay in when we can start the chemo. His first round of chemotherapy will be next Monday, Nov.14th.

We appreciate all the prayers, food, and support during this battle. We have been blessed by so many. The God of miracles is fighting with us and He will be glorified thru it all. Praise be to God!

We pray that you and your families have a Christ filled holiday season.

Prayer Requests
1. The chemo is able to completely eliminate what is left of the tumor in the next two cycles. Each cycle is 3 days with 4-6 weeks between. An MRI will be scheduled to check the progress.
2. The drugs do not cause side effects such as nausea, exhaustion, or any other symptoms (present or future) and he is able to stay on schedule.
3. As always we ask for prayer that God performs a miracle and the tumor is permanently eliminated supernaturally.

We are so grateful to have each one of you lifting our requests and family to the Lord!

👍❤️ 122   36 Comments 18 Shares

https://www.facebook.com/permalink.php?story_fbid=10154076815666245& id=251782711244

Prayer for Craig Davis
February 6, 2017 · St. Louis, MO · 🌐   •••

Praise God! We got relatively good news this morning. The tumor is still
there but it has reduced in size as a result of the chemotherapy. This is an
answered prayer because we were told that the type of tumor Craig has
doesn't normally respond. We also found out that there has not been any
spread down his spine. It wasn't quite the news that we all wanted, but very
positive. Regardless of what we were told His praise is ever on our lips and
our trust is in Him for Craig's complete healing. To God be the Glory!

 Heather McDaniel Speed, Clay Hahn and 152 others   33 Comments 20 Shares

https://www.facebook.com/permalink.php?story_fbid=10154324454626245&
id=251782711244

81

CHAPTER SIXTEEN: A Church 2,000 Miles Away

In February of 2017, I began to get a prompting from the Holy Spirit that I needed to take a step of faith for my physical healing. I felt strongly that we were to go to Bethel Church in Redding, California. I had listened to and sang many worship songs from Bethel music. As I mentioned previously, my theme song throughout this diagnosis and treatment was "Take Courage." But I wasn't familiar with the church and its leadership. In fact, I had never even heard of Bill Johnson. We didn't know anyone who went to church there. We didn't even know anyone who had ever visited there. So, it didn't make a lot of sense that we were being led to take off to this church that is almost exactly 2,000 miles from our home. But as it turns out, they have a heavy focus on supernatural healing and other miracles.

By this time, I believed in prayer for healing and I was comfortable with ministries that prayed earnestly for people to be healed. But, I was spiritually conflicted about modern-day signs, wonders, and even healing miracles. My only knowledge of and exposure to this area was through over-the-top television personalities. I had essentially dismissed the idea of modern-day signs, wonders, and instant healing ministries. For me, these types of healing ministries brought to mind images of people standing up out of wheelchairs, or reports of deaf people hearing, people growing out missing limbs, and so on. While I definitely believed in the power of prayer to bring healing, I didn't buy into the idea that people in the present day were able to pray over others to produce instantaneous healings.

Casey and I decided to take the trip and began doing some research. We found out that Kristene DiMarco was going to be at a local college for a worship night on a certain Friday, and that Bethel Church had healing rooms every Saturday where you could come for prayer. I was using a walker for getting around the house and a wheelchair anytime I left our home. Going to California with my physical limitations, in the middle of treatment, felt very daunting. Also, I still didn't know very much about Bethel Church. However, I had gotten clear direction from God that we needed to go. We did not really have extra funds in our budget to be able to go to California, but I went ahead and booked the flight and hotel room anyway. We also reserved seats for the worship night, which was thankfully a free event.

The next Sunday at church, a sweet lady came up and handed me a check which covered a majority of the trip. This incredible woman of God had always spoken healing words over me, but we had never discussed anything financial with her. Seeing that God was already moving in regard to this trip, we started to get excited:

Casey Davis is with Craig Davis.
February 16, 2017 · Eventbrite · 🌐

So super excited to be headed out to Bethel church in Redding California in just a couple weeks! I can't wait to see what God has in store as we go spend a few days just sitting in his presence.

Simpson University & **Kristene DiMarco** united in hope

It is Well

A free community worship and praise event

FRI., MARCH 3, 2017
7:30 PM

EVENTBRITE.COM
It is Well – Community Worship and Praise Event
Simpson University and Kristene DiMarco unite in hope to present "It is...

🔵🔴 Chandi Hester and 26 others   8 Comments 1 Share

https://www.facebook.com/casey.davis.1806/posts/10208546078344997

This morning, while preparing to write this part of the story, I reread the Facebook post I made on the flight home from Redding. I was brought to tears again while reliving the experience that I am about to describe. There have been other times when I felt the presence of the Holy Spirit, but nothing has come close to the experience I am about to share with you.

CHAPTER SEVENTEEN:
A Day at Bethel

When our plane landed at the small airport in Redding, the man that helped me off of the plane asked if he could pray for me. This was just a taste of the love and "hugs" from Jesus we would experience while there. We drove to the hotel and got checked-in. I was thinking that the city was not much bigger than my hometown of Tuscaloosa. We noticed palm trees, which excited Casey, and mountains in the distance. Palm trees and mountains seemed like a strange, but pretty cool combination. You can sense from our Facebook posts how excited we were to arrive:

Casey Davis is with Craig Davis.

March 2, 2017 · Redding, CA · 🌐

•••

We arrived in Redding and are super excited to go to Bethel! 😃 Always the first thing I do when I get to a hotel is diffuse some thieves to kill any germs that might be in here ready to attack us. I'm going to attack them first! I love thieves!

https://www.facebook.com/casey.davis.1806/posts/10208646965867122

Casey Davis is with Craig Davis.
March 3, 2017 · Redding, CA · 🌐

I didn't realize how beautiful it is here! I'm loving God's beautiful creation!

https://www.facebook.com/casey.davis.1806/posts/10208657015838365

Casey and I decided to find the church before the worship event that night in order to familiarize ourselves with the area. We noticed how beautiful the surrounding mountains were when we turned onto the road where the church is located. After a half mile, a large grayish-white church building came into view with plenty of snow-capped peaks in the background. Bethel is situated atop a fairly high elevation itself, so you can see for a long way in the distance on pretty much all sides. We parked and went to check out the inside of the church.

Immediately upon entering, a Bethel School of Supernatural Ministry (BSSM) student, who was also an employee at the church, introduced himself as Edwin and asked if he could pray for me. I guess it wasn't hard to tell that I was a cancer patient from my shiny bald head. The wheelchair was probably another strong clue that I needed prayer. He asked if we knew about the worship room, then asked if we would like to go. After grabbing a large "Prophetic Bear" at HeBrews Cafe, we found the worship room right where he told us it would be, just past the bookstore.

When we walked in, there were BSSM students and other church employees in a room that holds around 200 people. Some people were sitting while others were standing. A man was on a small stage playing soft worship music on his guitar. Everyone was either worshiping, praying, or reading their Bibles to "kick off their day," as Edwin had explained to us in the lobby. Another man came in and played the piano for about 30 minutes. Then they announced that the session was over and encouraged everyone to have a blessed day. What a fabulous way to start our trip!

We stopped by the bookstore on our way out, and I bought a book by Bill Johnson, the senior pastor at Bethel. I could not wait to find out the theology he preached and what the driving force was behind the tremendous passion we were witnessing. We went back to the hotel to get ready for the evening. I started into the first chapter of the book and was captivated by what I was reading.

The title of the book said it all: *When Heaven Invades Earth*. The premise of the book—that it is our role as Christ followers to bring God's will here on Earth—was a new thought to me. I had sung Bethel song lyrics which communicated this idea. But I had never thought much about what those lyrics meant to my daily life. I hadn't really considered the implications. God wants us to truly follow in the footsteps of Jesus so that He can bring not only the miracle of salvation, but physical healing into people's lives as well. Basically, God wants His people to live a life of miracles. Before we left for the worship concert, I read half of the book and a whole lot of Scripture just double checking all the things that I had been missing for so many years.

It was now time for the worship concert. We arrived to a packed-out gym at a small college in Redding. The college choir, along with Kristene, led a gym full of people in passionate worship for about two hours. As it was ending, we heard someone talking about going to the Friday late night worship at the church. Casey and I were all in at this point. We didn't want to miss anything. We went to get filled with more of the Holy Spirit.

The worship session was in the same room we had visited earlier that day. This time there was a full band on the stage and a packed room. I knew that God was preparing me for something big. What struck me about the service was the absolute freedom there. People were waving flags, dancing, and just lying down in worship. Just like David, they weren't hung up on what other people might think about them when they were worshiping the Lord.[4] I had never seen anything like it.

We worshiped until midnight and went back to the hotel exhausted—but eagerly anticipating what was to happen the next morning.

CHAPTER EIGHTEEN: Miracle Healing

We got to Bethel the next morning and followed the signs to the healing rooms, not really knowing what to expect. When we walked in, there were a couple of people sitting at a desk. They gave me a form to fill out, which had some questions about my sickness, whether I knew the Lord as Savior, if I had been baptized in the Holy Spirit, and so on. There were around 20 people already there. A few minutes later, a man came and told our group to follow him into the hallway.

There he explained the process and encouraged us to have faith in God for whatever we had come there for. Then he asked if anyone was there for back pain. A lady across the hall from me raised her hand. He went over to her and after comparing the length of her legs prayed for the shorter one to grow out. The reaction of the people around her told me something amazing had happened.

Even though I witnessed this with my own two eyes, I was hesitant to believe what I saw. I was very excited and trying my best to stay in faith, but I struggled with some doubt at this point. I could only think about how this had to be some kind of setup. Something was telling me the lady must have been planted there to perpetrate a trick on all of us. It was only later that afternoon—after I'd had the experience I'm about to describe and then seeing the lady again at the hotel—that I was convinced the lady was just a normal person like me who had come there for healing.

God does a lot of things that don't make sense to us. The Bible is full of stories that defy natural logic and that, quite frankly, seem weird to us. For instance, to be healed of leprosy, Naaman was told to go wash himself in a dirty river seven times. Sure enough, after the seventh time, he was healed.

Jesus rubbed spit on a blind man's eyes. The people watching may have thought he was crazy until the blind man could see. Another time, he mixed spit with dirt and rubbed it on someone to heal them. If someone did that today, we might label them as strange or even crazy. But, why? Because it's not the way we would do it? Because it looks weird? Because it doesn't seem credible? When searching for God's healing, it might help us to let go of some of our hang-ups.

When we were confronted with this lady's experience, my wife felt like God was saying to her, "Okay, either you're going to believe or you're not." That's what miracles do. They force us into a decision. There were a lot of people who still did not put their faith in Jesus even after seeing Him perform miracles.[5] Just like people in Jesus' time, we either choose to believe or we walk away doubting.

After the leg healing incident, I learned there was another group with around 25 people already ahead of us. After that group came out of a classroom, we were led into the room. A lady gave us a twenty-minute lesson about how much God loves us and how He desperately wants to see us healed and made whole. She pointed out how, in the biblical accounts, Jesus healed everyone that asked Him. Last, she gave us Scriptures that helped build our faith.

Next, we went into the main sanctuary. This was the first time I had been in there. I was surprised that it was not much bigger than the sanctuary of my home church. There were people in the middle of the room painting and dancing. A worship team was on stage singing softly as we prepared our hearts to go into the healing rooms. We just had to wait for the previous group to clear the room. I was nervous and excited all at the same time.

A short time later it was our turn. We went into the same room that we had worshiped in the night before. Now the chairs were cleared out, and there were groups of people scattered around the room, praying earnestly. A couple of students from BSSM came over and asked our names. They took the sheet that I filled out in the first room. They wanted to know more of my story. I gave them a 5-minute rundown of my first bout with cancer as well as describing the situation I was in now. I was in my wheelchair, which helped clarify my need. After reading Bill's book the day before, our worship experience the night before, and everything I had seen since we arrived, my faith was at a point where I knew anything could happen.

They brought us out into an open spot in the room and called a few people over. After asking if they could lay hands on me, they started praying. I do not remember the exact words or any of their names, but my neck felt like it was on fire. The prayer leader had everyone in the room stop and say, "Fire!" At one-point everyone around me, including Casey, took turns touching my neck and saying how hot it was on their hands. I knew beyond any doubt that this was the power of the Holy Spirit burning the tumor from inside my brain. I could feel it happening.

We went out in the hall afterwards to test whether I could do anything I couldn't do before. Since the healing could not be verified until my next MRI, I did the only thing I could think of and got out of my wheelchair and walked up the stairs. I still needed some assistance, but I was exercising my faith. Jesus often told people to do something before or after He healed them, so I didn't consider this strange. After hugging everyone we could see, we went into another room where we were taught not to let the enemy steal our healing. We were taught that he might try to deceive us into believing that what we felt and experienced in the healing room was not real. We walked out of the room and Edwin, the guy who greeted us when we first came in the church, was there waiting on us to see how things went and to pray for me one more time.

Here is a screenshot of the intro to a Facebook post where I told the same story a few days after it happened:

Craig Davis
March 7, 2017 · 🌐

Part 1 - Bethel Trip - Casey Davis

Our experience at Bethel was so much that I had to split it into two post. The one here that talks about why we went and our first few days and another that starts with the healing room. It was a blessed, anointed trip.

One day in early Febuary, after my morning worship time, I felt it in my spirit that a step was required of me. Some type of action that I would take to complete the healing that God has in store for me from this dreadful ...
Continue Reading

👍❤️ Casey Davis, Jacob Davis and 35 others   1 Comment 5 Shares

The full text of that post can be read here: *https://www.facebook.com/craig.davis.501/posts /10212059318455221*

If you read the full post, you may notice I had gotten past my hang-up about declaring my healing. I knew I was healed. I continued to declare my healing on Facebook all the way up until we got our MRI results two months later:

Craig Davis
May 5, 2017 · 🌐

Last night I was trying to put into words what hearing, "the tumor is gone" on Monday is going to feel like. That is how confident I am that the healing God has been doing in me is going to be revealed. I am not writing a post in case it's not or having a Plan B. I heard a wonderful analogy the other day in that the full armor of God has no armor in the back. Its purpose is for moving forward once you have direction from the Lord. I am only thinking and believing that the MRI that I had done last weekend is only going to show that no tumor exists. And when its shown how loud and audacious will my praise be to God. The proof that God's restoration to my body is beginning. The evidence of my Savior Jesus taking my stripes and healing me. All Glory to God!!!

🙂👍 Clay Hahn, Casey Davis and 85 others   20 Comments 2 Shares

https://www.facebook.com/craig.davis.501/posts/10212651826987564

If you go check out some of those Facebook comments, you'll see that a lot of other people were believing with me.

CHAPTER NINETEEN:
A Kingdom Focused Life

I was exhausted and still very excited after the healing rooms. As we were leaving, I noticed the parking lot was much fuller than when we got there. I thought about how amazing it would be to take part in these types of experiences every week. I thought about how wonderful it must be to operate as an instrument of God's purpose in the lives of His children. Our time in Redding up to this point had already given us much more than I ever dreamed possible. We went to lunch and looked at a few houses we found on Zillow, dreaming of what it would be like to live there. To say the least, we loved the palatable presence of God and we hadn't even been to a Sunday service yet!

Casey and I decided to arrive early at the 10:30 service. We wanted to grab some coffee and then soak up as much of the experience as possible. As we drove into the parking lot, the man directing traffic was dancing. I thought, "Wow! Even the parking ministry is fired up!" The parking lot was already packed. I knew that the auditorium would be packed as well after seeing its relatively small size the day before.

Casey went into the sanctuary and found that the only handicap spots were in the back. Just as we had seen in YouTube videos before we went, the front was packed with enthusiastic worshipers. The crazy thing was that the lady in front of us was one of the people who had prayed for me the day before in the healing rooms. She told me that she and her husband had prayed for me the night before when they got home. She also gave me some prophetic words of encouragement. The sanctuary was packed. There were people standing against the wall during this awesome worship service. The service was led by Eric Johnson, who is Bill Johnson's son.

Our flight home wasn't until the following morning. We knew that we would be coming to the night service and we resolved to get closer to the front and put my wheelchair in the back. I finished *When Heaven Invades Earth* that afternoon and had already resolved in my spirit that from this day forward, I was going to live a Kingdom-focused life. I was determined to bring God's supernatural reality into my daily walk no matter the cost or the risk. I immediately felt after reading the book that this was the primary purpose for my life.

At the night service, we saw baptisms going on during the praise and worship time. It was great watching people of every age, from young kids up to senior adults, being made new creations in Christ and celebrating with all of Heaven.

Baptism is one of the greatest moments, if not the best, in anyone's life and it was a privilege to witness this celebration while worshiping. Kris Vallotton preached that night. There was a lady sitting behind us who gave me another prophetic word. She basically said that she saw me standing on a hill, sword in hand, victorious in the battle I was currently fighting. Before we realized it, three hours had passed. As we would come to learn later on, this is typical for Sunday evenings at Bethel.

CHAPTER TWENTY:
Healing Revealed

It was semi-depressing when we had to leave, but we also really missed the kids. Knowing that I was already healed, I struggled to decide whether or not to finish up the chemotherapy treatments. Casey told me to do whatever was on my heart. Up to that point I had not experienced any significant side effects. Because of this, I decided to press on with the treatments, not realizing that my body had already had enough to harm me significantly.

The blood clots in my left leg started growing again and were causing more problems. I was having to take Lovenox shots twice a day, which was supposed to help keep the clots under control. In late April, the chemo really got to me. I was admitted to the hospital with a fever and a low white blood cell count. There was fear of infection, so I stayed a couple of days until I was no longer neutropenic—that is, until my body could fight infection again. Unfortunately, this happened all over again the next weekend. I believe that this was the enemy trying to put doubt and fear in me before the results of my upcoming MRI.

On May 8th, 2017, God revealed how awesome and mighty in power He is. As we were walking down the hall to get the results, I was full of faith. I knew that the tumor in my brainstem was gone. We didn't go to the same room where we had gotten the bad news about the cancer returning in 2016. This time, we were led into a different room and I remarked to my dad that this is the room where God's glory was to be revealed.

Dr. Campian was asking how I was feeling, and I cut right to the chase. I asked her to please just give us the results of the MRI. I couldn't wait to hear the news. She pulled up the images on the computer, and I verified with my own eyes that the tumor was gone before she ever said anything. I shouted, "Glory to God, it's gone!" She meandered a bit, seeming hesitant to give an official medical opinion that the tumor was actually gone. After all, according to medical science, this wasn't supposed to happen. But there was no denying the scan. She confirmed that the tumor was indeed gone, and I asked her if she could make a copy of the radiology report for me. I was ready to shout the news from the rooftops. I took no pleasure in "proving" the doctors wrong. My heart was just singing praises to the Lord.

There were so many people who had prayed for me over the previous year. They were eagerly anticipating the news that day, so I made a post on Facebook as soon as I had Wi-Fi. I had just witnessed the mountain get thrown into the sea, and I couldn't wait to share with my friends and family and for the name of Jesus to be glorified and praised.

 Prayer for Craig Davis
May 8, 2017 · St. Louis, MO · 🌐

The tumor is GONE!!! Praise Jesus! There are no words that I can say to express what my heart feels right now. The Lord has fulfilled and revealed what we knew to be true. He is the mighty healer! The doctor kept saying she couldn't say the cancer is gone forever but we know who we serve and He has healed me and I'm on my way to being restored. We will still do two more rounds of treatment to eliminate anything that's remaining and the fight is still on but we know its gone. We are just waiting for the final countdown. Praise the Lord and give Him ALL the Glory!
I just wanted to jump on and give a quick update so you all could rejoice with us and the mighty God we serve!!!

 308   121 Comments 56 Shares

https://www.facebook.com/permalink.php?story_fbid=10154572039421245&id=251782711244

On the same day, I also updated the part 2 of my Bethel experience Facebook post with a copy of the radiology report that says, "No evidence of residual tumor at the right pons. No new focus of disease." In English that means, "The tumor is gone!"

Craig Davis
March 7, 2017 · 🌐

Update: Today is May 8th and the healing God completed in my body that day in Bethel Healing Rooms has been confirmed. The water being poured into the bottle thru all the prayers and intercessions overflowed and Heaven invaded the earthly circumstances and the cancer was consumed by Holy Fire. Praise Jesus! We got the results of the latest MRI and there was no tumor and no sign of any disease. All Glory to God!!!

Part 2 - Bethel Trip - Casey Davis

Make sure you read part 1 ...
Continue Reading

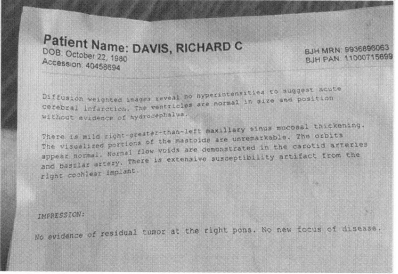

https://www.facebook.com/craig.davis.501/posts/10212059359896257

As you know, my cancer journey was somewhat captured on Facebook starting with the first diagnosis back in 2010, but the social media platform had grown exponentially since then, so we were now walking out our journey for everyone to see. There were so many people following the ups and downs and praying for our family that it was overwhelming at times. I cannot say it enough or truly express the importance of this, but we felt every prayer. We felt like there was a huge team behind us throughout every radiation session and every chemotherapy treatment. It was important for me to get the good news to my prayer warriors—and to give God glory as quickly as possible for the fulfillment of His promises. While I believe my healing was completed in Redding, I also believe that experience was a culmination of all the prayers that had been laid before God.

I had purchased another book by Bill Johnson before we left Bethel, *Releasing the Spirit of Prophecy: The Supernatural Power of Testimony*, and read it on the plane back to Illinois. I was realizing how important it was to tell others our God stories. In Hebrews 13:8, it says that *"Jesus Christ is the same yesterday, today, and forever."* (NLT) I wanted everyone to know that if He could do this for me, then He could do it for them—no matter how impossible their situation seemed. I wanted to tell everyone I saw.

I had promised God in faith that we would visit Him again on those beaches in Destin as soon as I was healed. I made the flight reservations and booked our stay at Henderson Inn. I started to get brave and tried to walk without my walker for short distances upstairs. Coming out of the bathroom, my left foot got stuck behind me. I had trouble walking normally because my left leg was still weaker than my right. I lost my balance and came down wrong.

I felt the break happen in my ankle. Casey and Tristen got me down the stairs eventually, and a trip to the ER confirmed it. We were supposed to leave for the trip in 10 days. Fortunately, both Southwest and Henderson Inn gave us refunds. We were disappointed, but we thought we would just reschedule after my ankle healed.

In July, we went in for a check-up that was clear, and I had Dr. Campian print side by side comparisons of the MRI images using the same view of my brainstem:

Craig Davis is with Casey Davis.

July 21, 2017 · 🌐

At my appointment yesterday I got these printouts at the doctor. One is the scan that was done right after the diagnosis prior to radiation and the other is the scan from a week ago. These visually show how big the miracle was and that it only could be done by God.

The cancer is recurrent grade IV Medulloblastoma, subtype Group 3. As you can see, the tumor was in my brainstem , which is what made it inoperable. At this point, the tumor had already shut down usage of my left side. I couldn't even wiggle my left toes and could barely move my fingers. You can also see there wasnt much room left before functons like swallowing, any movement, and breathing would shut down.

The best hope from my medical team, including a leading doctor in adult Medulloblastoma at Vanderbilt, was to contol the tumor thru radiation and hope that it goes dormant for a period of time with chemotherapy. Medically speaking there was no hope for recovery and if you ask the doctors then if I would be here today the answer would be no.

The Great Physician had other plans. As you can see from the scans from a week ago there is no tumor, not even a residual trace. The only way this could have happened is divine intervention, a miracle.

This is for anyone out there waiting on a miracle or questioning if God still does miracles. Put your trust in Him. Put your hope in Him. He is our Abba Father. He loves you more than you will ever comprehend. To God be the Glory!

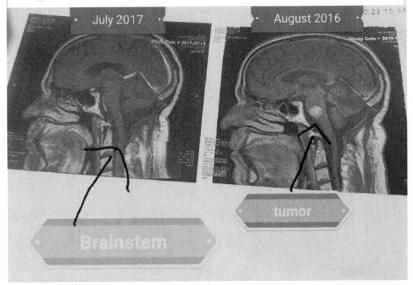

In August of 2016, the tumor is very clearly seen. At that time, I was paralyzed on my left side, and the tumor occupied almost all of the space in my brainstem. In contrast, the July 2017 image is completely clear with no sign of the tumor. This MRI image and the radiology report simply show the goodness of God and the compassion he had for me. He loves you and has the same compassion for you.

Before we got the chance to go to Destin, we enjoyed a family beach vacation in Gulf Shores, Alabama. I was gaining strength on my left side and my right foot was strong, so we considered it safe for me to drive again. I love to drive, even a minivan, so this was part of my restoration. I was believing God for complete restoration of everything that was lost—my hearing, my balance, my strength, etc. The enemy, of course, was out to destroy my confidence in my healing. I had no idea at that time, but another battle was ahead of me. The complete restoration process would have to wait.

CHAPTER TWENTY-ONE: Brokenness: The 3rd Diagnosis

In October of 2017, we got news that two small tumors had returned. One was in the same location as the 2010 tumor. There was also one in my brainstem. I was overcome with grief and exhaustion—tired of fighting these same battles over and over and over. My dad was up for a visit, and my friend Scott Wood came over to our house. I completely broke down with them in our prayer room at home. I was angry that the cancer was back for the 3rd time. I wondered why God had allowed it to happen, and I was scared that my death from this disease was guaranteed. The doctors did not tell me a treatment plan because the tumors were very small, so they were going to discuss my case at the next tumor board.

In that moment, I felt it was all hopeless because of how quickly the cancer had returned. It started to seem like no matter what I did, or how much I believed, or how hard I fought, the cancer was just not going to go away. I felt strongly that this was the end. I concluded that the healing from the large tumor in my brainstem was only to give me more time to say goodbye to my family.

I had thought a lot about my legacy over the previous year and a half. My legacy and memories with my wife as a husband, my kids as their father, and with my family and friends. I wanted to leave memories of someone who loved Jesus and walked out a faithful Christian life with joy and trust in the Lord. I got myself together as Scott and Dad prayed over me. In that moment, I knew that there was always hope in Jesus and that He hadn't brought me this far to let the devil win. I was mentally, physically, and emotionally exhausted, but somehow became determined to never give up. Here are some Facebook posts Casey and I made from that day:

Craig Davis is with Casey Davis.
October 19, 2017 · O'Fallon, IL · 🌐

Everyone has those days where you know the events will shape your life's direction. It could be the birth of a child, the day you got married, got accepted to a college, or when your school won a championship (or many) or the day you sat in a doctor's office getting results from a test or scan. I know many of us have been in those offices for various reasons. I want to say that I've become immune to the anxiety and stress these visits cause, but then I would not be being honest with you. But one thing I am certain of, as we get ready to go, is that my God already knows the outcome, the Holy Spirit will be present with me, and my Jesus will be there to hold me and comfort me. I have been healed and saved by the redemptive blood of the cross and my life is His. I choose to walk out my journey on the other side of the cross.

And I am convinced that nothing can ever separate us from God's love. Neither death nor life, neither angels nor demons, neither our fears for today nor our worries about tomorrow—not even the powers of hell can separate us from God's love. No power in the sky above or in the earth below—indeed, nothing in all creation will ever be able to separate us from the love of God that is revealed in Christ Jesus our Lord.
Romans 8:38-39 NLT

To God be the Glory,

Craig

 Clay Hahn, Ginger Watkins Roberts and 66 others   21 Comments 1 Share

https://www.facebook.com/craig.davis.501/posts/10214245007296076

Craig Davis is with Casey Davis.
October 19, 2017 · O'Fallon, IL · 🌐

The news today was not good. A tumor has come back in the location of the tumor in 2010. My medical team will be meeting on Monday to discuss options. We should know Tuesday or Wednesday whether surgery, more radiation, or more chemo would be possibilities. My heart is weak right now with thoughts of leaving my family overwhelming me. I will process this and look to the Father to try and find the strength to face another battle.

 Clay Hahn, Anthony Estes and 73 others   86 Comments 8 Shares

https://www.facebook.com/craig.davis.501/posts/10214247017026318

Craig Davis is with Casey Davis.

October 19, 2017 · O'Fallon, IL · 🌐

• • •

I appreciate all the love, support, and prayers being shown to my family. This has been a tough day for all of us, but I knew thru experience with this dreadful disease that it had returned before we went to the doctor. My heart hurts for all the sacrifices my precious kids and my beautiful wife will endure. My physical body hurts in anticipation of another round of surgery, chemo, or whatever gets thrown my way.

But as I sit here tonight I am at peace. It's a peace that truly surpasses understanding. My God is good. He didnt give me this disease to because He thinks I can handle it or to test my faith. Any strength and courage I have comes from the Holy Spirit. He loves me and I can feel His love in the depths of my soul. Even as I ask why and my emotions are questioning everything.

The fact is we live in a broken, fallen world. Tragic events and accidents happen all around us. Brave men and women lose their lives fighting for us. Children die from diseases and cancer everyday. This is not our home.

Jesus made a way for me to be born again into His family. I am a son of the King and a brother of the risen Savior. I will fight this disease with everything I've got and whether He calls me home during this struggle or 50 years from now I will praise the Father and seek to glorify Him in everything I say and do. My trust is in Him.

To God be the Glory,

Craig

 114   32 Comments 8 Shares

https://www.facebook.com/craig.davis.501/posts/10214250478352849

113

https://www.facebook.com/casey.davis.1806/posts/10210366080243907

I had another MRI about a month later to see how quickly the tumors were growing and to determine an action plan. We decided to have the gamma knife procedure and then do a stem cell transplant. A gamma knife procedure is just extremely focused radiation that is used for smaller tumors. The stem cell transplant involved extremely high doses of chemo to get my blood count low and then put my own healthy stem cells back into my body.

Casey and I arrived for the gamma knife procedure, and the team moved quickly. Dr. Kim's time is precious as a neurosurgeon, and we all wanted to get this done. They had gotten an image of the exact location and custom fitted a metal head mask for me. The doctor arrived, telling me that he and a nurse were going to numb my skull to screw the mask onto my head. He told me it would feel like a bee sting and he was partially right. I said that those were the worst, meanest bees on the planet because the numbing shots in my skull hurt like crazy. I guess it's better to be numb than to feel metal screws going into the bone. I looked like Bane from the Batman movie, *The Dark Knight Rises:*

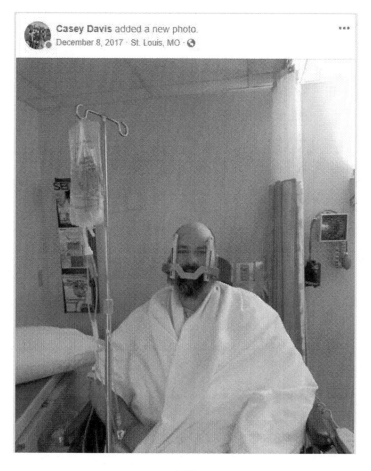

The rest of the procedure was relatively painless. I believe that, again because of all the prayer covering, I did not experience any of the side effects. I would just have to wait until after the transplant to see how effective the procedure turned out to be. We would have to give the radiation time to work on the tumor.

You may wonder, "Why didn't you guys just get on another plane to Redding?" While my experience and encounter at Bethel was significant and life-changing, neither myself nor anyone at Bethel believes that God's healing is only available there. I do believe they have an anointing, and I love Bill Johnson's teaching. But that trip was the result of a prompting from the Holy Spirit to go to Bethel at that specific time.

Later on, I went to a conference at Kansas City and had Bill Johnson sign my book. It told me a lot that when I had the opportunity to tell Bill Johnson about my healing at Bethel, he acted like it was a normal event. Of course, he was happy for me, but healing reports are common there. I look forward to the day when they become common in my ministry.

CHAPTER TWENTY-TWO:
Stem Cell Transplant

Our family enjoyed another Christmas together as we prepared for the stem cell transplant. We knew that a minimum 4-week stay at the hospital was required and we had made arrangements with friends and grandparents to keep the kids. The older kids were in school and the younger boys were still at home. Casey rarely left my side through all the procedures and treatment. She said there was no way she was leaving me alone now. We didn't realize how tough the transplant was going to be on us.

We went in on January 15th, 2018, for the transplant. Everything started quickly after our arrival. I had a central line put in because my port was not capable of handling that much chemo at one time. I would begin the regimen that night. Because I was also getting steroids and nausea meds, sleep was at a premium the first week. There was a chemo drug in my treatment that I'd never had before. This drug is largely excreted through the skin, so I was required to take a shower, change clothes, and put on new bed sheets every six hours, day and night. The plan was to administer the chemo for the first eight days, have two rest days, and then introduce the healthy cells on day ten. Medically, this is called "day zero" for a stem cell transplant.

The enemy threw everything he could at us during this time. Our van broke down and had to go in the shop for repair. Our kids were getting sick and everything at home felt chaotic. You feel helpless in that situation because there is no way you can leave. Once the process starts, you cannot leave the hospital for any reason because you are susceptible to any and every type of infection under the sun. As you can see from this Facebook post, my wife is an amazing prayer warrior who wasn't having any of it:

Casey Davis is with Craig Davis.

January 28, 2018 · 🌐 ···

I believe the enemy was trying really hard to take Craig out yesterday because that's what he does. God's word says The thief (satan) comes only to steal kill and destroy BUT I (Jesus) have come that they may have life, and have it to the full. John 10:10

I believe God released miracles in this room yesterday, In Craig's body. He was here in the midst of the chaos releasing peace like only he can do, releasing healing like only he can do, and releasing love like only he can do. He pushed back every fiery dart the enemy tossed at Craig. The Lord is strong and mighty in battle and no one can stop him! He is such a good good father. Things shifted as we all prayed and believed God to do what only he could do yesterday. I just stood around his bed worshiping God for who he is. Just because he is good, he is faithful, and he loves Craig. In the midst of all the chaos he is still good and he calmed the storms around us. He is a miracle working God!

Keep praying because God's not done yet! He is much much better but still really sick. He wants to totally heal and restore Craig and I'm believing for just that!

Thank you all for praying and believing with me. We love and appreciate you all so much!

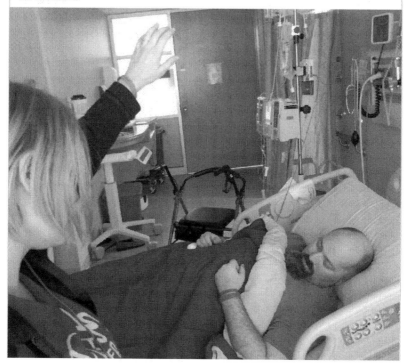

We are also blessed with amazing friends and brothers and sisters in Christ who helped us through the issues. More so, we were blessed to have Jesus right beside us throughout the entire experience. We knew that we would need Him more than ever when all the medications started to catch up with me.

With the first two doses of chemo, I lost a significant amount of hearing in my left ear. I was already unable to hear out of my right ear due to previous treatments. On the third dose, I lost all of my hearing. I had to use a whiteboard to communicate with Casey and the nurses. My strength and energy were wiped out. I was nauseous most of the time and also dealing with horrible mouth sores. I ate very little and was receiving fluids and blood transfusions as needed. We were praying for improvement.

On day zero, when I received the healthy cells, I began to feel a little better. I no longer had to shower every six hours. Also, I knew that the Lord was answering my prayers because I began to hear a little. It is easy to take our senses such as sight, touch, taste, and sound for granted until we begin to lose them. My hearing and taste had suffered tremendously, and the feeling was terrible.

Siteman had built another wing to the center, and I was one of the first patients to occupy the new transplant wing. The hospital staff was still working out the kinks in the rooms, but my room had a wonderful view of Forrest Park in downtown St. Louis. I was still dealing with terrible fatigue, but my energy was slowly coming back.

CHAPTER TWENTY-THREE:
The Value of Christian Relationships

My brother in the faith, Scott Wood, visited with me every day to pray over me and bring me food. He knew I probably couldn't eat most of it, but he wanted to bring it anyway just in case I could. My small group from church moved our weekly meetings to my room at Siteman. They even put on "space suits" for me because those were required for entering my room the first couple of weeks.

One day I woke up to find Pastor Rick just hanging out on the bench by the window. Dad was there whenever he could be, and he took the boys to Tuscaloosa for a few weeks. My mom was going to come when we left the cancer center and stay for a few weeks to help with the transition back into our house. Of course, Casey never left my side, except to get food from the cafeteria or run quick errands. She was my rock as usual, and I know she brought Heaven into that room every day. Finally, after 31 days I was going home.

Over the next month, I had a few hospital stays for infections. They were not pleasant, but my immune system was so battered that even the slightest germ or virus would result in fevers. I was determined to get through this and begin the restoration process that I knew God had in store for me.

CHAPTER TWENTY-FOUR:
Cancer Free!

On June 5th, 2018, we received the news that there was no sign of cancer. I heard one of the top neurosurgeons in the country tell us that my scans looked great. I was declared cancer free! Praise God! My restoration back to full health was beginning.

The next day I booked our trip back to Destin to fulfill the promise we made to God two years prior. As a reminder, that's where we had told God we would return to the same beach to praise Him for my healing. I understood, now, that last year the battle wasn't over yet. The time had not yet been right to visit those sandy shores. But now it definitely seemed like the right time.

I got a little over the top wanting to celebrate life. While talking with my dad, we decided to do a family vacation in Orange Beach after Destin. At the same time, Casey and I planned a cruise to celebrate our 20th wedding anniversary in September because I had been in the hospital for the stem cell transplant on the actual date of our anniversary.

On the flight to Destin, I fought back tears. I was very emotional because of what this trip signified to me. Casey and I were about to be in a place where we encountered the Holy Spirit in a very powerful way two years before. We received promises on those sandy beaches and spent intimate time with Jesus, being comforted and prepared for the battle ahead. Henderson Inn represents a sacred milestone in my life. It makes me think of the Old Testament, when they would put up altars in a certain place to remember a significant act of God.

This trip was a time of celebration and thanksgiving. We told our story to anybody that would let us grab their attention for a few moments. God helped us out with the weather being perfect, and we held each other—reimagining our future together with our family. We shared what the Holy Spirit was telling us about our future serving the Lord. We felt like He was telling us that there are no limits with Him.

There is no limitation to where He might take us or the things He can do in and through us. I had been thinking of the difficulty in selling our house and moving the kids. I realized I had been placing limits on Him. He totally removed those and other constraints from my mind. Our lives are committed to Him to do whatever He calls us to. I simply want God to be glorified, not just for what He has done for me, but for who He is. Like the song says, He is a "good, good Father."[6]

Before cancer struck back in 2010, I was a Bible-believing Christian. I could answer most theological questions. I taught kids in Sunday School and adults in small groups. I knew that Jesus was my Savior, and I did my best to be kind, compassionate, and giving in my daily life.

Now I look at my life as a Jesus follower from a different perspective. Knowing Him and the heart of the Father is my singular pursuit. My life is His and I am no longer placing any limits on what He can do through me. Nothing is impossible!

CHAPTER TWENTY-FIVE:
Lessons Learned

O ver the course of the last couple of years, I have learned, tried, and encountered things that have helped and others that have hurt. The good practices helped me to build my faith and ministered to me in times of doubt and fear.

Ever since the trip to Bethel, we have been looking for times of spiritual refreshing whenever I was physically able. Our awesome friends went with us to Kansas City to visit IHOP—the International House of Prayer, not the breakfast restaurant. We also made it to a Bethel Conference. We got to worship with awesome praise teams and hear Bill and Eric Johnson preach and pray over us. That was the trip I mentioned earlier, when I got Bill Johnson to sign my copy of *When Heaven Invades Earth*. That book completely changed my perspective on what it means to be a Christ follower.

Later we attended another Bethel conference in Dallas with our close Christian brother and sister, Eric and Juliana Staub. We also go to other events in our local area. These events put me in a place of focused praise and worship of God in a large corporate setting. This inspired me and motivated me to continue to press into God and to glorify Him, not for the gifts He has given me, but just for who He is. It's a different dynamic than Sundays or with your small group at home. The time there is set aside for focused prayer and teaching where you can be refreshed.

In addition to my daily (I at least try every day) quiet time activities of reading the Bible and praying, I have incorporated other practices. I believe that speaking God's promises from Scripture out loud was vital to my healing and my spiritual health. Speaking the truth of His Words aligned my spirit with the Holy Spirit and helped me physically, emotionally, and spiritually. I meditated on healing Scriptures and spoke them out loud as well.

I had a pamphlet from Charles Capps called "God's Healing Hands," which is full of Scripture. I wore that pamphlet completely out as I went through it speaking Scripture over myself. My wife bought me another copy, and I've just about worn that one out too. It's very important to meditate on, pray, and declare God's promises over ourselves and our situations.

Some mistakes that I've made allowed the enemy to deter me from walking in complete faith during the journey. I did not immediately take sinful thoughts, such as worry and fear, captive in accordance with Scripture. This allowed the enemy to put doubt and lies into my mind, causing further fear and anxiety. While worshiping at our small group one night, I was convicted of this and repented from my fear.

By "repent" I do not mean beating myself up about weaknesses and shortcomings. Instead, to repent means to turn away from wrong thoughts, feelings, or actions. I would turn completely around and act the way Jesus wants me to act. He always wants what's best for us. As the lyrics of one of my favorite songs says, "My fear doesn't stand a chance when I stand in Your love."[7] You must continually guard your heart and mind against these thoughts. Otherwise, they can be crippling.

Also, if you walk out your journey on social media, you'll need discernment as you read comments and messages from well-intentioned brothers and sisters. To those walking beside someone who is battling cancer, I would advise avoiding certain things. For example, it's best to help by praying, encouraging, and serving people in this situation. Advice and instruction to someone dealing with a deadly disease should only be given after a lot of prayer, some wise counsel from others—and still with great caution even after you've done those things.

I believe that God's desire is to heal everyone this side of Heaven. Jesus never turned down anyone who asked for healing in faith. I believe you must walk in the faith that what you ask God for, He will provide. If you believe that everything is inevitable and predetermined, then prayer would be futile, and hope would be useless. God's love for us is too immense. We put our lives and trust in His hands, and He wants to give us good gifts.

If you believed God was the cause of sickness as well as healing, then you would believe in a God who was doubleminded and warring against Himself. Sickness does not originate with God, but rather from the curse of sin—the very thing Jesus came to redeem us from! God is a good, perfect Father who created the world and humanity as a perfect paradise. Wholeness and healing is what He wants for us.

Does everything always turn out the way we want? No. Even as I write this book, we've just suffered the loss of Casey's brother. Casey also recently had her own health issues and ended up getting a hysterectomy. Obviously this world is not perfect, but you must believe in your spirit that everything is being used for your good. You must believe, as Isaiah Chapter 38 demonstrates, that your situation can be changed when you pray. God already loves you and is full of mercy toward you, so the deck is stacked in your favor.

CHAPTER TWENTY-SIX: Reflecting Back and Looking Forward

I have come to know God more deeply through experience and encounters with the Holy Spirit over the last nine years. Probably more so over the last two and a half years. I look back at the career opportunities lost, dreams that were broken, and the physical limitations I have, and I think to myself almost daily that knowing Him more intimately is worth all of it!

He is my joy. I've discovered a love in Jesus and experienced the power of God and His goodness that I wouldn't trade for anything. This journey has changed me in ways that I never saw coming. I treasure the little things in life because I now know how precious life is. My sons' first steps. My daughters' first bike rides with no training wheels. Those rare dates with my wife. These little things now often bring me to tears.

I've seen, met, and read about other patients— some with the same disease—who pass away, and I wonder at times why I am still here on this earth. Why am I not in Heaven with Jesus? I know my two boys would not be here if He had taken me home in 2010. I know that people's lives have been touched by my story. If one person comes to Christ and gives their lives to Him, then all of the pain, difficulty, and heartache are worth it. The pain, the fear, the anxiety, and the sacrifice of what I dreamed my life would be like when I used to put that Air Force uniform on each day—it has all been worth it.

I have found a joy and peace that only Jesus can give. Whatever happens from here, whether I have a terrible accident, the cancer returns, or I live to be 80, I have found the greatest treasure of all— my place in the family of God. I am a son of the Most High God, and I trust Him with my life and my family's future.

*"Here's what I've learned through it all: Don't give up; don't be impatient; be entwined as one with the Lord. Be brave and courageous, and **never lose hope.** Yes, keep on waiting—for he will never disappoint you!"* – Psalms 27:14 (TPT)

To the Reader

First of all, I am honored that you took the time to read this story of what God has done in my life. I believe with all my heart that He can do the same in your life—no matter your situation, health concern, financial concern, or relationship problems. He loves you more than you know. I'd like to end with a prayer over you.

Prayer

Lord Jesus, I thank You for my healing, but most of all I thank You for saving me and allowing me to be in right standing with the Father for all of eternity. Thank You for offering me a way into Your family. I know that You love me more than I can comprehend. Holy Spirit, I pray that You give the reader hope and peace in whatever their situation might be. In an instant, You can change any circumstance they might be facing. I pray that You do the impossible in their lives. If they don't know You, Jesus, and the salvation that You have for them—to save them out of an eternity separated from God—I pray that today they choose You as their Lord and Savior. Free them from the chains that are holding them back from an intimate relationship with You. I pray this in Your precious and holy name.

Amen.

Request from the Publisher

If you enjoyed Craig's story or found it helpful and encouraging, would you please consider leaving an honest review on Amazon and other websites? When you take just a few moments of your time to do that, you help us—more than you could possibly know—to spread the message of hope and healing to those who need it. Also, please be sure to tell others who you think might benefit from Craig's book. Thank you so very much for sharing in Craig's story and his ministry.

Appendix: Story Extras

There are many more details—many more moments of pain, challenge, loss, restoration, joy, and victory—that we could not fit into the book. So, we thought some readers might find it helpful to see other parts of the story that played out on Facebook. This is not an exhaustive list, but these are some of the moments that stood out in our minds as being significant:

1) My wife, Casey, reflecting on our first Destin trip when we cried to the Lord and He ministered to us: *https://www.facebook.com/casey.davis.1806/posts/10206952886556198*

2) My daughter's 12th birthday celebration from the hospital: *https://www.facebook.com/photo.php?fbid=10211203214491740*

3) Me walking with my friend, Scott Wood, in the hospital and longing for home: *https://www.facebook.com/story.php?story_fbid=10211129644772543&id=1099603441*

4) Casey posting about a visit from the kids and giving updates:
https://www.facebook.com/story.php?story_fbid=10211104355180319&id=1099603441

5) Someone set up a meal train for us:
https://www.facebook.com/story.php?story_fbid=10210836201196637&id=1099603441

6) Finding a way to have fun, we took a spontaneous road trip to see an Alabama football game on my birthday:
https://www.facebook.com/story.php?story_fbid=10210377962540957&id=1099603441

7) Casey remembering a previous victory and declaring full restoration for me in Jesus' name:
https://www.facebook.com/story.php?story_fbid=10210273951860755&id=1099603441

8) A post about our visit to IHOP and a Bethel event in Kansas City:
https://www.facebook.com/story.php?story_fbid=10213073720734644&id=1142108856

9) Decision to stop chemotherapy:
https://www.facebook.com/story.php?story_fbid=10212908379841225&id=1142108856

10) I made a decision to be more intentional about sharing my heart and my thoughts on Facebook: *https://www.facebook.com/craig.davis.501/posts /10210938309830706*

11) My next post after deciding to share more on Facebook: *https://www.facebook.com/story.php?story_fbid= 10210943428318665&id=1142108856*

12) Picture and post with extended family at Grace Connection Church: *https://www.facebook.com/story.php?story_fbid= 10207458106041189&id=1544213545*

13) Heaven on my mind: *https://www.facebook.com/story.php?story_fbid= 10210130131026741&id=1142108856*

14) A warrior for Christ: *https://www.facebook.com/story.php?story_fbid= 10209897035959510&id=1142108856*

15) My near-perfect life in the months before the second diagnosis: *https://www.facebook.com/story.php?story_fbid= 10206423506242021&id=1099603441*

16) My reflections on wrestling with God after the second diagnosis:
https://www.facebook.com/craig.davis.501/posts /10210998096845344

17) Casey reflecting on how God was with us in each moment:
https://www.facebook.com/casey.davis.1806/pos ts/10210320428662646

18) We often prayed, and asked others to pray, very specific prayers:
https://www.facebook.com/permalink.php?story_ fbid=10153933304366245&id=251782711244

19) God had a book planned all along, but I was trying to share my story however I could:
https://www.facebook.com/craig.davis.501/posts /10212748176036230

20) Jesus Christ is the only way to Heaven:
https://www.facebook.com/craig.davis.501/posts /10211095110630628

Immediately before final publication, we noticed something really interesting in one of Casey's Facebook posts from January of 2017. She had gone to the treatment floor at Siteman and was reflecting on the tiles painted by patients, their family, and their friends:

About the Author

Craig Davis, a former Airman in the Air Force, learned a new kind of warfare while battling brain cancer three times. He utilized traditional medical treatments in addition to studying and using the Word of God to fight his battles. Now his mission is to help others overcome the challenges they face, so he wrote *Never Give Up Hope: Waging War With Cancer* to encourage and strengthen people who are in difficult situations.

Craig also enjoys sharing his testimony in person. He is available for interviews, public appearances, and speaking engagements. Please contact Called Writers Christian Publishing for more information.

Craig was medically retired from the Air Force in 2011. He holds a BS in Computer Science from Saint Louis University and an MBA from Fontbonne University. He lives with his wife, Casey, and their six children in the greater St. Louis area. They are donating all of their proceeds from the book to various ministries and charities.

References and Notes

[1] "What is getting an MRI like?" *YouTube*, uploaded by Via Christi, 27 April 2012, https://www.youtube.com/watch?v=DZTXa4qerI4. Referenced comments are found at time = 4:00 – 4:09.

[2] "Medulloblastoma." *MayoClinic*, https://www.mayoclinic.org/diseases-conditions/medulloblastoma/cdc-20363524. Accessed 21 November 2018.

[3] "Adult Medulloblastomas." *NCBI*, https://www.ncbi.nlm.nih.gov/books/NBK12737/. Accessed 21 November 2018. The number we cite is calculated from the incidence rate given by this source. The incidence rate is .5 per million according to NCBI, and the number of adults in the U.S. is 245 million according to the U.S. Census Bureau.

[4] "2 Samuel 6:16-22 English Standard Version." *BibleGateway*, https://www.biblegateway.com/passage/?search=2+Samuel+6%3A16-22&version=ESV. Accessed 21 November 2018. This sentence is referring to an account of David given in 2 Samuel 6:16-22.

[5] "Matthew 11:20-21 New Living Translation." Bible Gateway, https://www.biblegateway.com/passage/?search=Matthew+11%3A20-21&version=NLT. See Jesus' statements recorded in this passage for a clear example.

[6] "Chris Tomlin - Good Good Father (Audio)" *YouTube,* uploaded by christomlinmusic, 2 October 2015, https://www.youtube.com/watch?v=CqybaIesbuA.

[7] "NEW SONG: Stand In Your Love – Josh Baldwin | Live From Heaven Come 2018." *YouTube*, uploaded by Bethel Music 19 July 2018, https://www.youtube.com/watch?v=oFizRY8w0-I.

54755376R00093

Made in the USA
Columbia, SC
06 April 2019